# TEA THROUGH CULTURE

*Strategies for reading and responding to young adult literature*

**Joan Parker Webster**

Arte Público Press
Houston, Texas

*For my parents, who were
my first teachers.*

This volume is made possible through grants from the City of Houston through The Cultural Arts Council of Houston, Harris County.

*Recovering the past, creating the future*

Arte Público Press
University of Houston
452 Cullen Performance Hall
Houston, Texas 77204-2004

Cover design by Giovanni Mora

Webster, Joan Parker.
    Teaching through Culture : Strategies for reading and responding
    to young adult literature / by Joan Parker Webster.
        p.   cm.
    ISBN 1-55885-376-6 (pbk. : alk. paper)
    1. Young adult literature, American—Study and teaching.
2. Young adult literature, American—History and criticism—
Theory, etc.   3. Pluralism (Social sciences) in literature—Study
and teaching.   4. Young adults—Books and reading—United
States.   5. Ethnic groups in literature—Study and teaching.
6. Youth—Books and reading—United States.   7. Culture in
literature—Study and teaching.   8. Multicultural education—
United States.   9. Race in literature—Study and teaching.   I. Title.
PS490.W43 2002
810.9′9283′071—dc21                                        2002066668
                                                                        CIP

♾ The paper used in this publication meets the requirements of the American National Standard for Information Sciences—Permanence of Paper for Printed Library Materials, ANSI Z39.48-1984.

2 3 4 5 6 7 8 9 0 1                    10 9 8 7 6 5 4 3 2 1

# Contents

# Preface

Learning to read is perhaps one of the most highly publicized, researched, and debated topics in the field of education today. The topic of reading has become prominent in the political arena as well, securing its place as a national priority steeped in rhetoric and promoted through legislation. To be sure, the ability to read is one of the most important processes that must be developed by students if they are to be successful in school and beyond. That is the primary reason why I decided to write this book. But, this book is not about the often highly politicized debate over which approach or what program is the best to accomplish this goal. Rather, this book is about helping students negotiate the process of reading and comprehending texts, which has at its center the ultimate goal of constructing meanings from texts. The word *meanings* is used with careful intention, because texts can contain and generate many different *meanings*. Readers, therefore, can be influenced by what a text says—its actual content—as well as what a text says to them—the coming together of textual content and the reader's background knowledge. What makes the interplay of these two elements—what the text says and what texts say to a particular reader—important to constructing meaning? Simply put, if a reader cannot find a way to connect the ideas presented in a text with her or his own knowledge base and life experiences, the possibility for the reader to construct meanings may be seriously constrained. Both of these elements are integral parts in the process of comprehension.

## The Relationship between Reader and Text

The idea of a dynamic relationship between text and reader is not new. Reader response theorists have described the different roles that the reader and the text play in a reading process that is fluid and constantly unfolding (Bleich, 1975; Iser, 1978; Rosenblatt, 1978; Fish, 1980). Despite there being variations in degrees of the contributions by the reader and text (and authorial intention) toward constructing meanings, the reader is foregrounded in the process of making meaning.

This view of reading and responding to literary texts has driven and continues to drive instruction and assessment in many of our classrooms, and I agree with an approach that allows for agency on the part of the reader and the recognition of different perspectives in the creation of meanings. However, I think it is important to consider some additional factors that come into play when implementing this approach to reading literature, particularly in the context of today's diverse classrooms, which reflect a multiplicity of cultural, linguistic, racial, and ethnic backgrounds.

When we ask students to read a piece of literature, we need to recognize the integral part that understanding what the text actually says plays in the process of comprehension. If the reader has no understanding of what is happening in a story at this very basic level, she or he may have no point of departure from which to engage the text, and there may be a disconnect in the relationship between the text and the reader. This can result in a break in the process of comprehending that depends on a reader's engagement with the text at this primary level. Thinking in terms of how this piece fits with what a reader brings to the text, it seems necessary that in order for a connection to be made, the reader must be able to find a hook on which to hang his or her prior knowledge and life experiences. For many students whose cultural, linguistic, racial, and ethnic backgrounds are different from the dominant culture reflected in most school curricula, a text that lacks any connection to anything in their lives can and often does subvert the process of comprehension at the very outset.

This can be devastating in a testing climate that privileges a view of comprehension based on the ability to restate what the text or reading passage says as interpreted by those constructing the tests. We cannot therefore underestimate or ignore the need for the reader to understand what the text actually says. Understanding the text then is the mediating part of the process of comprehending that provides readers with the means to interpret what the text says to them.

This leads to another key factor in fostering the process of comprehending—choosing the texts. The act of choosing a text with its socially and culturally constructed content can be considered a way of reproducing culture, because literature is part of the larger sociocultural context, historically positioned in time and place. In other words, literature is a cultural product or resource (Leitch, 1992; Fiske, 1989). Looking at literary texts as cultural documents then, it could be said that when reading and responding to literary texts, readers, who are also cultural beings, positioned in time and place, are actually involved in the study of culture (Rogers, 1997). This seems highly important when we talk about readers making connections to texts, because choosing and using materials that foster these connections rests at the center of a culturally responsive pedagogy. No doubt, most educators would agree with the axiom that learning requires building on prior knowledge and background experience of the learner. If this is true for learning in general, how much more appropriate is this concept when we think about choosing texts and developing strategies for reading and responding to literature? But, equally important, given that the study of literature implies the study of culture, is the recognition that we need texts that present other than the dominant culture in our schools' curricula. This brings me to why I chose the particular texts that are the focal points for discussion and the basis for implementing various reading and writing strategies in a literature-based classroom.

## Choosing the Texts for This Book

The Latino population in the United States has been on a

steady increase over the last decade. According to the 2000 Census data, in states like Arizona, California, New Mexico, and Texas, which share historical roots in Mexico, it is not surprising that the Latino population between the ages of five and seventeen constitutes a major portion of the overall population, ranging between 34 and 42 percent. However, in other states, such as Colorado, Illinois, New Jersey, New York, and Rhode Island, the growth of school-age Latino population is also rapidly on the rise.

Overall, according to summary data from the 2000 Census, approximately 16.2 percent of today's youth between the ages of five and seventeen are Latino, and three out of four of approximately ten million students with linguistically diverse backgrounds are Latino students (NAEP, 2000; NCES, 1997). This trend, marking a shift in the dominance of cultural groups reflective of Anglo/European backgrounds, suggests the need for a shift in the choice and use of literature and curricular materials if we are to keep up with these significant demographic changes in the student populations of our schools.

The need for the inclusion of literature reflecting the pluralistic society in which we live has been a clarion call made over the past several decades by educators who advocate multicultural education and cultural responsiveness in curriculum and instruction. The recognition of the need for making multicultural literature an integral part of the school curriculum and instruction is important for two reasons. The first, as stated previously, is the need for texts that reflect the culture of the reader in order to facilitate the construction of meaning by acting as a mediator between students' experiences and literacies that exist outside of school and those that are part of the culture of schooling. However, equal, if not more important, is the need to create a school environment that is based on social justice, which values and empowers all students. For, if students continually see only one culture, which is predominantly mainstream, white, and middle-class, reflected in the literature they read, then this becomes the norm against which all "other" people are viewed. Such a myopic view of culture can have a damaging effect on all students. For those students within the dominant culture, a lack of exposure to other perspectives can seriously limit their ability to question the status quo and hinder their development of a critical stance toward the social, political, and economic systems that influence our daily lives. Students outside the dominant culture, who see no images of themselves, or inaccurate portrayals of their culture in the literature that they read in school, can experience a devaluing of their cultural identities. This can result in a loss of self-esteem and empowerment that can seriously limit agency, which is a key ingredient to learning. It is with these two primary reasons in mind that I have chosen the literature included in this book. But, in addition, the selection of these young adult novels reflects choices of quality literature that can stand on their own as good examples of the art and craft of storytelling about the human experience, and, as such, should be part of any literature-based classroom.

## Overview of the Chapters

I will now introduce the chapters and text selections that form the basis for the reading and writing strategies presented in each chapter. The unifying feature of all the selections is that they can be categorized in the genre of fiction. Two of the novels, Cofer's *Silent Dancing: A Storyteller's Memories* and Rivera's *And the earth did not devour him* both provide examples of the heritage of an oral tradition in which the storyteller collects and preserves the memories of a people and their culture. Two novels, *Jumping Off to Freedon* (Bernardo) and *Trino's Choice* (Bertrand), are contemporary stories about male protagonists involved in life-changing, real-life dramas that mirror events that are happening in our world today. Lachtman's *Call Me Consuelo* combines mystery with a subplot centered in identity issues and a young girl's coping with a new environment. And, *Spirits of the High Mesa* (Martínez) blends a family's and community's history with the historical events of the period just after World War II to illustrate the dichotomous nature of progress. When I first read the novels, their strong underlying themes seemed to suggest naturally a frame for the strategies I developed for reading and responding to the stories. However, although the strategies are thematically linked to the corresponding stories, each strategy can be adapted and applied to other texts used in your classroom instruction.

Chapter 1, "Becoming a Culturally Responsive Teacher," provides an introduction to the notion of *culturally responsive pedagogy* and explores the different teaching methods developed in specific cultural contexts. Also in this chapter is a discussion about the importance of using culturally appropriate materials and the need for teachers to develop a critical stance toward choosing literature for use in their classrooms. A brief overview of the five sections that organize each chapter is also presented.

Chapter 2, "*Silent Dancing:* A Storyteller's Memories," studies Judith Ortiz Cofer's stories based on her childhood memories as she and her family migrated back and forth between the island of Puerto Rico and the mainland U.S. in Patterson, New Jersey. The primary theme of storytelling is the main focus of the strategies described in this chapter. However, strategies based on ethnographic methods to develop detailed images of places and people that make the stories are also presented. To extend the story into other content areas, strategies that connect to the rich and varied history of Puerto Rico are outlined. The strategies employ a variety of techniques that incorporate different oral and written formats, which work together as a multi-genre response to the reading.

Chapter 3, "*Call Me Consuelo:* Mystery and Subplot" examines Ofelia Dumas Lachtman's story of Consuelo, a young girl whose parents died in a car crash. After living with her aunt and uncle, she must move away from her Spanish-speaking family and friends to live with her Anglo grandmother in the big city, where she becomes involved in solving a mystery. The strategies in this chapter are based on good mystery-writing techniques designed to develop synthesizing and hypothesis-forming skills. There are also strategies that explore the subplot, which works to portray the issues of separation, alienation, and identity that are experienced by many children who must adapt to new linguistic and cultural surroundings.

Chapter 4, "*Jumping Off to Freedom:* Fiction from Today's Headlines," works with a story similar to that of many Cuban rafters who have risked their lives to "jump off" to freedom for a better life in the United States. The strategies in this chapter, like the book, reflect the two primary settings where the action of the story takes place—in Cuba, before escaping, and on the raft at sea. There are also strategies designed to examine the underlying historical and political events that have influenced and continue to influence Cuban and United States' relations, which directly affect the people living in Cuba today.

In Chapter 5, "*Trino's Choice:* The Power of Words," we study a book about a teenager who must face some very important choices that can affect the rest of his life. Some choices can lead him into dropping out of school and, possibly, a life of crime—a life in which others tell him what to think and do. Others open up possibilities in which Trino can have the power to direct his own life. This power of words—being able to read and understand them, and being able to express oneself through words—is the primary framework for the strategies in this chapter. There are also strategies designed to take an ethnographic look at the different social groups represented in the school context and community resources that provide good choices for out-of-school activities.

Chapter 6, "*Spirits of the High Mesa:* In the Name of Progress," explores the notion of change and how many things sanctioned in the name of progress can have devastating effects on people as well as their environment. Strategies in this chapter focus on the literary elements of plot—how plots are developed and the kinds of conflict that are essential to creating a good story. There are also strategies centered on character development and the techniques an author uses to create a strong, *round* character who grows and changes throughout the story. Extensions to the theme of the story focus on issues of protecting our environment for future generations.

In Chapter 7, "*...y no se lo tragó la tierra/And the Earth Did Not Devour Him:* Voices of the People," we find a collection of narratives that exemplify the heritage of the oral tradition. The narrator in the novel, like the oral storyteller, relies on the collective memory of a people to reconstruct and retell their cultural history so that it can be passed on to future generations. The striking element in this novel is the way Rivera represents the voices of the culture through his skillful use of different narrative structures that incorporate dialogue, dramatic monologue, and different points of view. The strategies in this chapter focus on these literary devices as well as the use of verbal and situational irony. Strategies are also built on authentic dramatic representations of the text, since the dialogue in many of the episodes closely resembles that found in the improvisational skits associated with Chicano theatre.

In the final chapter, "The Story Continues," I summarize the connections between the stories themselves and suggest ways to adapt and use the strategies presented in the chapters to other literature studies. Finally, I look forward to new possibilities for creating environments for culturally responsive learning that are situated in communities built on an ethics of caring (Noddings, 1992, 1984).

## Reading the Text

*Teaching through Culture: Strategies for Reading and Responding to Young Adult Literature* is about teaching, but it is also about learning, because teaching and learning are inextricably tied together. Thus, teachers and their students are on a collaborative journey in this lifelong endeavor of teaching and learning. The importance of this collaborative relationship rests in a socio-constructivist theory of learning, which suggests that knowledge is constructed within social interactions (Vygotsky, 1978; Wertsch, 1991). It is within these interactions or communicative actions (Habermas, 1983; Carspecken, 1996) that we negotiate meanings as we contribute our perspectives and listen to others', which can open up possibilities of coming to new understandings. The concept of negotiation through collaboration is an important one and is at the center of Vygotskian theory. This also forms the basis for Vygotsky's (1978) *Zone of Proximal Development* (ZPD). In Vygotsky's perspective, the ZPD is a space in which children can achieve a learning goal that might be beyond their present knowledge base and task experience. However, I think this applies to *all* learners. As human beings we are continually encountering new experiences that present thresholds for learning. These thresholds are spaces similar to what Vygotsky described as the ZPD. As teachers and lifelong learners, we find ourselves traveling through these spaces, along with our students. It is in these spaces that we can assume different roles. At times, we are the more knowledgeable collaborator, providing the scaffolding for the other learner. Yet, I believe, even as we are the active scaffolder, as reflective teachers we are also learning through this experience. At other times, we may be the one who is being scaffolded through new territory. Many times a comment or even a question by a student has opened the door to a new threshold of learning for me, pushing my thinking beyond where it had been a moment before. This reciprocal and collaborative relationship, then, seems integral to what we term cultural responsiveness in both teaching and learning and should direct our paths toward the negotiation of meanings and understandings in the classroom and beyond. It is my hope that through reading and responding to the literature presented in this book, both you and your students together will experience the power of teaching and learning through culture.

# Chapter 1

# Becoming a Culturally Responsive Teacher

## Introduction

In classrooms today, all over the United States, the numbers of culturally, racially, ethnically, and linguistically diverse students are steadily increasing. A good friend who teaches in an elementary school in Anchorage, Alaska, recently told me that in her school alone there are fourteen different home languages other than English represented in the student population. What does this mean for teaching and learning in such diverse contexts? For many students whose backgrounds differ from the mainstream culture that dominates most of our schools' curriculum, instruction, and assessment programs, this can and does mean low academic performance. This achievement gap, as it sometimes referred to by many educators, is a complex problem that is often viewed through one lens, the standardized test score, which identifies these low achievers. Unfortunately, this identification mark is a negative sign that often leads to the conclusion that it is the student and her background that are responsible for this failure to "make the grade." A complete discussion of the issues underlying standardized testing is beyond the scope of this book (for discussions on this subject see Coles, 2000; Taylor, Kohn, 2000; Murphy, 1998; and Calkins, Montgomery, Santman, 1998). However, suffice it to say, this unilateral approach to assessing student learning and achievement in schools does not provide the teacher or the student and her family with an accurate measure of what the child knows or is capable of doing.

In the university classes that I teach, there is a great deal of discussion about the advantage students have when they come to school with prior experiences involving children's books and being read to at home. These students seem to be more equipped with the skills needed to be successful in school, for obvious reasons. Their home literacy experiences contribute to the child's preparation to learn in a school culture because they are primarily based on the same kind of literacy. In other words, the literacy at home is the same as the literacy taught at school. But, what about those students who don't come to school with this kind of background experience? Are they devoid of literacy experiences? The work of Heath (1982) and others has of course shown that there are many different kinds of literacies that children bring to school with them. The question then becomes how do we as teachers build on this knowledge in such a way that children continue to develop these multiple literacies rooted in their cultural orientations and at the same time become successful in the literacy practices that are part of the culture of school? The numerous discussions that have developed in response to this question are centered in what has been called a culturally responsive pedagogy (Gay, 2000).

## Defining the Term

*Culturally responsive pedagogy* is one of a number of similar terms that all relate to improving teaching practices by making them more compatible to the different cultural, racial, ethnic, and linguistic orientations of students. These terms have sprung out of research into teaching methods used in culturally specific contexts. For example, Au and Jordan (1981) referred to the instructional methods used by teachers instructing native Hawaiian children in reading as *cultural appropriateness*. Mohatt and Erickson (1981) used the term *culturally congruent* to describe the style of teacher-student interaction that was most successful for teachers of Native American students. *Culturally relevant* teaching uses the student's culture as a way of maintaining that culture as well as overcoming the negative effects of the dominant culture of schooling (Ladson-Billings, 1994). A "culturally responsive" teacher, then, fosters students' cultural knowledge, builds on their prior experiences, and employs appropriate communication and interactional styles to engage students in learning.

The state of Alaska has taken the notion of cultural responsiveness in teaching to another level through the creation of *Standards for Culturally Responsive Schools*. Developed by Alaska Native educators as a complement to the state's content standards, the standards for culturally responsive schools are designed to shift the focus of curriculum and instruction to a more in-depth study of the surrounding physical and cultural context in which the school is located. The standards also provide for the recognition of the unique contributions to knowledge that indigenous people can make in these teaching and learning communities. Thus, through this shift in the focus in the curriculum from teaching and learning *about* culture as a discrete content subject, to teaching and learning *through* local culture, all ways of knowing, forms of knowledge, and worldviews can be recognized as equally valid (Alaska Native Knowledge Network, 1998). While these standards were designed for rural schools serving Alaska Native students, the focus seems applicable to all students and communities.

## What Is Culture?

If we are to become culturally responsive teachers, perhaps we should begin with an understanding of the complexity of this term. Simply stated, culture encompasses the values, beliefs, traditions, and worldview of a group of people who are bound together by physical location, common language, history, socioeconomic class, or religion. But, culture is not a monolithic object that stands outside of the human experience, nor is it directly visible. It can, however, be observed and tacitly inferred, and it is often manifested in our social behaviors, ways of interacting through speech and nonverbal gestures. Culture, then, is a dynamic organism that is socially constructed by human beings. As such, it is also influenced by social, political, and economic systems. Consequently, culture is in continual flux. Clifford Geertz (1973) described culture as being fashioned through a public dialogue that people enter to negotiate continually established meanings. This continuous dialogue contributes to the overarching cultural narrative as well as to the individual stories that are part of the whole. Stories, then, are an important way for us to proclaim ourselves as cultural beings; the way we craft our stories and their very content are evidences of our cultural membership (Dyson, Genishi, 1994). Schools are places where cultures meet, and, consequently, they are places where we can tell our stories and listen to other stories, and even transform ourselves through these stories. Like culture, which creates a frame of reference for our lives through its organization of space and time and values (Lipka, 1998), stories too provide a way for humans to organize their lived experiences into important events and happenings. We are all members of a culture or cultures, and we all have stories to tell.

## The Importance of Culturally Relevant Texts

In my work with teaching immigrant children and young adults how to read and comprehend English texts, I have found that using literature that provides cultural connections for the students to be the most successful way to engage these learners actively and improve their comprehension. When students can see themselves in the stories they read, it often serves to provide a needed handhold on familiar territory in the often overwhelming and intimidating environment of school. Reading texts that are culturally relevant provides pathways to prior experience and knowledge. As teachers, we all know and have experienced the importance of accessing and building on prior knowledge as a key ingredient to the process of comprehending texts. Equally important, however, is the opportunity that is presented for students to "scaffold" the teacher's and other students' learning, acting as the more knowledgeable expert about their culture. The reader, in talking about a text that is relevant to her or his life, becomes the storyteller who takes the printed text off the page and transforms it into his or her own. In this way, students can continue to build upon their cultural and experiential knowledge and at the same time develop in the literacy practices that are part of the culture of school.

## Multicultural Literature in the School Curriculum

How do we determine cultural relevance in texts? The term *multicultural literature* is often used to refer to literature by or about groups who have been marginalized in the dominant society. Historically, this has meant groups such as African Americans, Latinos, Asian Americans, Native Americans, and Alaska Natives, and a variety of others, such as women, gays and lesbians, the elderly, the disabled, and religious groups. However, many view the label of multicultural literature as inadequate and even problematic. If we define multicultural literature as of or about *the other*, meaning those other than white, middle-class citizens of the United States, we are using the dominant culture as a standard or norm of comparison, and are thus, reinforcing the social patterns that have been reproduced for decades (Harris, 1997). Nieto (1992) describes multicultural education as being for *all* students and as a way for schools in our society to respond appropriately to a democratic pluralism that *is* our country. In this view, reading literature that is written by and about the many different or *multi*cultural groups that are part of our pluralistic society can be a way for students to maintain and affirm their culture and also learn about cultures other than their own. Reading multicultural literature can also be a way for students to examine critically the historical, social, political, and economic influences and their effects on different cultural groups in our country.

Adopting a critical stance is also important when choosing and using *any* literature in the classroom, for teachers as well as students. In a recent master's level children's literature class, composed of practicing teachers, a genre study approach was used. The purpose of the class was to review and critically evaluate young adult novels for incorporation into school curricula. Students read books individually, and some books were read in literature circles. Most of the teachers in the group had used literature circles in their classrooms as a part of their literature-based curriculum. In the course, we studied the traditional literary elements of the texts and the history, trends, and characteristics of each genre. Reading texts through the lens of various critical literary theories—New Historicism, Feminism, Psychology, Deconstruction (Soter, 1999)—was also explored. However, an overarching analytic stance that examined the author's relationship to the culture being portrayed and non-literary elements, such as stereotyping, omission, historical inaccuracies, portrayal of power relationships, and so forth (see Slapin, Seale, 1992), was emphasized for reviewing and assessing the novels. As the class progressed, I noticed an evolution in the kinds of discussions about the various texts. At the outset, most of the literature circle groups began talking about books in the way they approached teaching with literature circles in their own classrooms. That is, they discussed some of the literary elements of the novel, but concentrated more on their personal responses. Then, as new theories and evaluative criteria were introduced, the conversations took on a tone that emphasized the critical analysis of the texts, particularly the portrayal of the cultures represented in the books. The conversations still included personal responses; however, these were more backgrounded. This was no doubt a natural outgrowth of the progression of the content being presented in the course. However, the striking thing about the evolution of these discussions can be summed up by a student's comment that was iterated by all of the class members: "After this class, I will never be able to look at a book in the same unquestioning way again. This will affect how I choose books and the ways I will teach them."

In summary, then, the inclusion into the curriculum of multicultural literature that accurately and respectfully portrays the culture being presented is necessary to provide students with an undiminished view of our pluralistic society. But, by inclusion I do not mean additive, in the sense of a special unit of study, outside of the *regular* curriculum. Rather, I am advocating the use of quality children's and young adult literature that is written by diverse authors, representing *multi*-cultures as part of the curriculum being implemented every day in our classrooms. After all, a good story is a good story and can be told from many perspectives through diverse voices. This is the underlying assumption upon which the present book is based.

## Reading the Novels

Using literature circles as a way for students to read and respond to texts is one of the best approaches to reading the novels highlighted in this book, simply because it allows for greater interaction and talk about the books. If you are unfamiliar with this approach to reading literature, there are several models that outline specific jobs and responsibilities for the members of the group (see Daniels, 1994; Samway, Whang, 1995; Short, Pierce, 1998). The basic format of literature circles consists of small groups of four or five students that meet together on a regular basis to read and discuss young adult novels. Each member has a job within the group. For example, one student may facilitate the discussion, while another may identify unknown vocabulary words for the group. As you read through each chapter of this book, you will find prereading, during-reading, and post-reading activities in the different sections of the chapters. Depending on the experience level with literature circles, group members can be assigned the responsibility of facilitating the different activities. If you have not used literature circles before, these activities can also be presented and demonstrated through whole group presentation, followed by small group discussion and collaboration.

## Chapter Sections

In each chapter, there are sections that are common to all chapters. These contain information that provides background as you prepare to read the novels and strategies to help students as they read and respond to the different texts. While the strategies for each novel are geared toward the story's content, each strategy can be adapted for use in teaching other literature selections or other curriculum content areas. The five sections are: *Synopsis of the Story, Building Background before You Read, Reading and Responding to the Story, Working with Words,* and *Connecting across the Curriculum.*

## • Story Summary

Each chapter begins with a brief summary of the plot of the novel, including a description of the principal characters. This section gives teachers information that can help in curricular planning.

## • Building Background before You Read

To help set the context for the story, important background information is given to aid the teacher in preparing students to read. The information provided is not meant to be all-inclusive; rather it serves to highlight key points that can be examined further as extensions to the story. For example, in Chapter 4, "Jumping Off to Freedom: Fiction from Today's Headlines," a brief summary of the historical and political events leading to the establishment of Fidel Castro's government in Cuba provides a backdrop to the story about present-day Cuban rafters who risk their lives to escape this oppressive regime.

## • Reading and Responding to the Story

In each chapter there are different prereading, during-reading, and post-reading response strategies to help students construct meaning from the story and enhance their comprehension of the text.

## • Working with Words

Strategies designed to build vocabulary are presented in this section. Some of the strategies are based on words taken from the story. Others are based on a key element or theme. For example, a key event in Chapter 5, *Trino's Choice: The Power of Words,* is centered on the genre of poetry. Since a primary tool of the poet is the use of descriptive words, the focus of the strategy is on developing descriptive language that contains rhythmic and melodic sound qualities.

### • Connecting across the Curriculum

The strategies in this section link the story content in each novel to activities based on various content curriculum areas. For example, in Chapter 2, *Silent Dancing: A Storyteller's Memory,* students research and develop a museum of artifacts that tell a story of Puerto Rico's history and people.

Many of the teaching and learning strategies suggested in these sections rely on an inquiry approach. This approach is an effective way to engage actively the learner in a topic of his or her interest through which higher level-thinking skills are developed. While the inquiry approach to teaching and learning has been defined and interpreted in many different ways, these iterations all share some common assumptions. These include a view of the learner as active, with a natural desire to explore and question the phenomena of her world; of creativity and self-expression as natural outgrowths to learning; and of social interaction and communication as a mediator for learning. I view inquiry as a process through which students can better understand their world, and teachers can develop understanding of the students they teach and their own practices in the classroom. Thus, student inquiry and teacher inquiry can operate in tandem and support each other within a classroom community of learners. Thinking in terms of a K-W-L chart (Ogle, 1986, 1989) that has been traditionally used as a research tool in content area units, the students identify what they *Know* about a topic, then what they *Want* to know (based on unanswered questions), and finally what they *Learned.* However, the process is also recursive, and at any stage may be revised and reformulated. This inquiry process seems similar to the process of teacher action inquiry, with the added element of building on the newly acquired learning by posing new questions, thus beginning the cycle again. The example in Figure 1.1 illustrates the parallel nature of teacher and student inquiry processes.

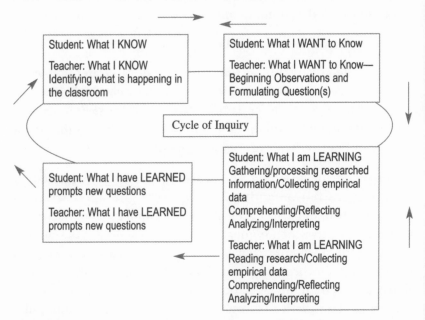

**Figure 1-1.** Parallel Nature of the Cycle of Student and Teacher Inquiry

## Developing Your Approach to Culturally Responsive Teaching

Becoming culturally responsive to the needs of diverse learners is not a matter of having a bag of instructional tricks that are pulled out on special days or thematic units highlighting a cultural group. Developing as a culturally responsive teacher requires building a set of attitudes, values, and understanding that guides your decisions in your daily instructional practice. As such, educators at all levels must continually maintain a reflexive stance. In this stance, the teacher as learner involves herself in a recursive process of understanding the phenomenal world and at the same time examines the way this developing understanding changes his or her relationship to that world and how it is being observed and understood (Tripp, 1998). In other words, reflexivity is more than an evaluation of whether a lesson accomplished a set of goals. It also, and perhaps more importantly, involves an examination into how those goals fit with one's developing and changing ideas and attitudes about teaching and learning. As teachers who are also involved in inquiry into their own practices, this seems a key element in improving our instruction. As you prepare to read this book, start by brainstorming your own beliefs about teaching to diversity. Think about how these beliefs are manifested in your classroom instruction. Are there evidences of teaching practices that coincide with your stated beliefs?

Finally, developing a culturally responsive approach to teaching requires that educators recognize the relationship between traditional school-based knowledge, culturally-based knowledge, and the affective realm in learning. Fostering a balance in this relationship allows educators to build on the multiplicity of interests, different forms of knowledge and ways of knowing, and worldviews that are represented in the pluralistic society in which we all live.

# Chapter 2

## Silent Dancing:
## A Storyteller's Memories

### Story Summary

*Silent Dancing: A Partial Remembrance of a Puerto Rican Childhood* is a collection of "cuentos" or stories told or recounted by the author that are based on memories of her childhood. For Cofer, these memories are the points of departure for her stories of strong, emotional connections to the people, places, and events that have danced in and out of her life as she and her family migrated between the island of Puerto Rico and Patterson, New Jersey. Cofer introduces the reader to memorable Island spaces, such as Mamá's house with its many rooms and La Escuela Segundo Ruiz Belvis, the "color-coded" school. There are also spaces on the mainland, such as El Building, La Bodega, and P.S. 11. Through these spaces move characters that are family members, friends, and acquaintances whose stories fill the pages with joy, sadness, love, contempt, pity, envy—those universal forces that define us as human.

The reader enters a world rooted in the oral tradition that serves to entertain and teach through stories with lyrical and rhythmic lines. Each story is followed by a poem (in some cases, two poems) forming a kind of complementary coda for the preceding descriptive, almost poetic narrative. Both story and poems demand to be read aloud. We learn through the eyes and ears of the narrator about the power of story, and that the language used to build stories is the only weapon against the power of authority (p. 66). Through her cuentos, Mamá exercises her "matriarchal command" and holds the power to cast a spell over her listeners (p. 15). And, it is Mamá's voice that "convinces Cofer of the power of storytelling" (p. 19). Within Mamá's stories are lessons in what it means to be a woman. They draw from women's tragic experiences of becoming a victim of love, like María la Loca, and glorious, triumphant experiences that speak of transformation through love, like María Sabida. Cofer also spins her tales of women, who like María la Loca, have made choices that provoke feelings of contempt or pity. However, Cofer points to the underlying strength that each of the women exhibits despite her ill-chosen fates. For example, the beautiful young woman Vida is admired by the young narrator of the story, who through her admiration becomes "the little pocket mirror she could take out at any time to confirm her beauty" (p.105). Vida leaves her family and her aspirations of a career in Hollywood for a man whom her family does not approve of, and she moves in with the narrator's family. Soon she begins to exhibit bad habits. She does not help with housework nor contribute to the household finances, and she always wears the heavy scent of alcohol and generously applied cologne. Then, suddenly, Vida is gone. The story of Vida closes with an image of her face on a poster announcing her win of a Catholic parish beauty contest. The caption "Vida wins!" (p. 109) sums up the underlying strength of Vida, who, despite poor choices in love, exercised her strong will to accomplish a long sought-after goal.

The story "Silent Dancing" from which the book takes its title, is a testament to the need for story and the power of words. The story is actually told through three scenes in a silent home movie, which used to be a popular way of documenting family memories and special occasions. Unlike today's VHS video and digital camcorders, this type of film recorded usually grainy images, without any sound. Cofer provides the reader/viewer with the words that complete the preservation of the memories and, more importantly, the identities of the women and men in the film. In attaching words to the visual images, the narrator also attaches power that can only be found in language. In the last scene, people are seen dancing in a circle. For years, reveals the narrator, "I've had dreams in the form of this home movie" (p. 95). In her dreams, each dancer steps forward to tell a brief and cautionary tale that gives voice to the past and teaches to the future. Without this language, there is only silent dancing that reduces the dancers to "absurd" and "frantic" images with incomplete memories and powerless, silenced identities.

## Building Background Before You Read

## Puerto Rico: Its History and People

The island of Puerto Rico is part of a large archipelago containing more than 7,000 islands that is known as the West Indies. Among the other islands within this archipelago group are smaller groups of islands that form the Bahamas, the Lesser Antilles (Barbados, Trinidad, Tobago are part of this group), and the Greater Antilles. Puerto Rico is located in the Greater Antilles group, along with Cuba, Jamaica, and the island of Hispaniola, now divided into the countries of Haiti and the Dominican Republic. Archaeologists have found evidences of habitation of different groups of people on the island during pre-Columbian times. Sailing in large canoe-like boats, the Igneris, primarily fishermen from the Orinoco River region of Venezuela, settled in what is now Puerto Rico. The Taínos, believed to have been Arawaks who migrated from South America, followed them. The Taínos lived on the island they named Borinquen—Land of the Regal Lord—for nearly 1,000 years before Cristóbal Colón (Christopher Columbus) and the Spaniards arrived. When Christopher Columbus first landed on the shores of Borinquen and Hispaniola, he encountered the Taínos, a highly organized people who had no written alphabet and, consequently, rather than recording their history and myths through written language, they memorized them and passed them down from generation to generation through storytelling. The near extinction of the Taínos made the handing down and, thus, the survival of original Taíno history, myths, and legends nearly impossible. However, second-hand written accounts of Taíno myths and religious beliefs do exist, primarily due to missionaries who recorded them in Spanish. Some cultural artifacts and words such as *hamaca* (hammock) and *barbacoa* (barbecue) have come down to the present, but very few real vestiges other than physiological features in the people remain today.

By the early sixteenth century, the Taínos were nearly extinct due to disease and inhumane treatment at the hands of the Spanish explorers and colonists. After 1511, because of the decimation of the Taínos and the ongoing need for a labor force on the island, African slaves were brought to the island to work in the fields and provide brute labor for the development of the Spanish colony. Although African influence was somewhat weakened through Spanish assimilation, the African contribution to the island's cultural traditions can be traced through the food, music, dances, and cultural practices that are still part of the island culture. Even some words were incorporated into the Spanish vocabulary: words like *bachata*, which means party, *mofongo*, which is a culinary dish made of plantains, *guingambó*, which is similar to gumbo in Louisiana are some examples.

Spanish rule of Puerto Rico lasted until 1898. As a result of the victory over Spain in the Spanish-American War, Puerto Rico was ceded to the United States as part of the Treaty of Paris, and the Island became a possession of the United States. This essentially exchanged one colonial power for another. Puerto Rico has remained under the colonial rule of United States since then. In 1917, with the implementation of the Jones Act, the people of Puerto Rico were made citizens of the United States. It was not until 1952, however, when Puerto Rico was granted "commonwealth" status, that self-rule comparable to that of a state of the Union became a reality. This allowed Puerto Rico to govern itself, like a state, and elect its own leaders, but not to have representation in Congress or conduct international business and relations like a sovereign country. Since 1952, there have been ongoing debates involving different political factions on the island. Generally, these groups are divided into those who favor statehood, those who want to become a free republic, and those who want to continue as a commonwealth of the United States.

The folktales and stories being told in Puerto Rico today still reflect many cultural themes introduced through Spanish colonization and acculturation beginning in 1493. However, these themes are also overlaid with adaptations from the Island's multicultural fabric that have been woven together over the past 500-plus years. Puerto Rico has many folktales that reflect the diverse voices of the island's past and present inhabitants. Tales such as the humorous antics of the picaresque Juan Bobo, as well as stories based on natural phenomena, such as the song of *el coqui*, the little tree frog that is indigenous to the island, are all part of the storytelling tradition that is a central to *Silent Dancing*. An example of this rich folktale tradition is found in the tale of "María Sabida," the legendary folk heroine who was "wiser than any other woman on the Island of Puerto Rico, and her name was known even in Spain" (p. 74).

## Migration: Life in Two Contexts

Other stories reflect the more recent Puerto Rican experience. As previously stated, because of the enactment of the Jones Act in 1917, the people of Puerto Rico became citizens of the United States. As U.S. citizens, residents of the island could legally migrate between Puerto Rico and the United States mainland. This movement, often referred to as *migration,* as opposed to immigration, has contributed to both linguistic and cultural maintenance and a high rate of bilingualism and biculturalism for many Puerto Rican people (Nieto, 1997). A primary reason for migration to the mainland U.S. was to seek better economic opportunities. Initially, many Puerto Ricans migrated to New York and then began to move to other neighboring northeastern states like Connecticut and New Jersey. Early migration began during World War I, when the factories and shipyards of New York needed labor. Heavy migration began in the 1940s, when again Puerto Rican labor was needed to abate the manpower shortage during World War II. In this context and in new roles, they faced discrimination and exploitation, suffering harsh working conditions, substandard housing and low wages, similar to the experiences related in Rivera's ...*y no se lo tragó la tierra* (see Chapter 7). The trend in recent years toward a downturn of factory and farm industry jobs in the United States, brought on by industries relocating to other countries where even lower wages are allowed, fewer and fewer relatively good paying and secure low-skill jobs are available. This, along with relatively inexpensive air travel to and from the Island to the mainland, has created a circular pattern of migration, which has resulted in a cultural and linguistic maintenance and a resistance to assimilation into the dominant U.S. culture. This lack of assimilation through cultural and linguistic continuity is a much different experience than that of earlier immigrants to this country (Nieto, 1993).

This concept of a circular migration pattern is reflected in the stories of *Silent Dancing*. The *cuentos* and their characters move back and forth between the island and the mainland United States. In the opening story, Cofer's narrator describes herself as a navy brat, "shuttling between New Jersey and the pueblo" (p. 17). Later, she reveals that her family lived in Puerto Rico until her brother was born. Soon after, because of "economic pressures," her father joined the U.S. Navy and was stationed in the Brooklyn Navy Yard. Leaving the island first, her father found housing in El Building, a tenement building where other Puerto Rican families lived. Cofer paints vivid pictures of life in the city, contrasting the neighborhoods of cement and steel in shades of gray to the bright airiness of the island's tropical environs. As Cofer's characters migrate between the two settings, readers will not only experience the varied physical surroundings, they will also travel on an inner journey of changes occurring in the characters that are brought on by differences in the social and cultural environments.

## Reading and Responding

A well-crafted story combines the various literary elements—plot, character, setting, theme, and style—in such a way that all work together to create a unified whole. In *Silent Dancing,* Judith Ortiz Cofer accomplishes this unity through the brief storied moments of memory recorded in each chapter with its accompanying poetry. Since the book is based on story and storytelling, this is the main focus of the activities outlined in this chapter. However, the activities are also influenced by another interesting aspect of the book, namely, Cofer's style, which incorporates a multigenre approach. This style blends folktale, personal memoir, poetry, and what seems to me a type of commentary very similar to ethnographic research journaling found in the italicized notes about the film segments found in the "Silent Dancing" chapter. As you read the book *Silent Dancing,* the following response activities can be implemented either in small literature circle groups or as a whole class. The activities incorporate different genre and writing formats such as reader response journals, poetry, personal memoir, biographical sketches, and historical research. The activities also include some ethnographic methods to collect information such as site/room maps, observational notes, and interviews. Since ethnography is, in the broadest sense, concerned with studying and describing human phenomena and the cultural basis for the different ways we live, the use of ethnographic tools seems parallel to the idea that Cofer introduces in the "Preface." For Cofer, writing a personal memoir may stem from a need to study ourselves. When we study ourselves, we also study those people who are a part of our lives, both past and present. As you work through the following activities, keep a portfolio or file of the various responses to the text. These can be combined into a multigenre collection.

## Tracing Migration in the Stories

Migration plays an important role in the lives of many of the characters in the book, particularly the narrator's. Before you begin to read the stories, ask this guiding question: What are some of the issues that the main character faces as she moves back and forth between different physical and cultural environments? Then, as you read, trace this migrating movement and how she feels about each environment. For example, Cofer describes herself as a navy brat who moves between New Jersey and the island "pueblo" (p. 17). In this passage, she reveals that her peers made her feel like an "odd-ball," making fun of her "two-way accent," speaking Spanish with an English accent and English with a Spanish accent. We also discover the difference between the two environments. In New Jersey, the narrator's mother keeps her children under "strict surveillance," and life is portrayed as restricted and confined. In contrast, on the island, Mamá frees them "like pigeons from a cage." Divergent images such as these are woven throughout the stories.

Two important places in the two environments are home and school. Readers can trace these contrasting images by recording how they are described and what moods or feelings are evoked. Begin with collecting the physical descriptions of the environment from text. Then find passages that relate to or imply social, political, and/or cultural issues. For example, consider the explicit example like the issue of English taught as a foreign language versus English as the only language of instruction found in "Primary Lessons" (p. 54). Other passages contain more implicit connections to issues and may require inference on the part of the reader. For example, in the passage about schooling at P.S. 11 (p. 65-66), the author describes what it was like as a predominantly Spanish speaker with limited proficiency in English to attend a school with English as the only language of instruction. Embedded in this description is the issue of instruction in English only versus bilingual or English as Second or Other Language (ESOL) programs for students who come to school with a first language other than English. Finally, ask readers to reflect on their own experiences by comparing the text to their lives. Some students may have had similar experiences to those of the author of *Silent Dancing*. Others may have had experiences with the linguistic issues of instruction and can relate how they fit with the programs offered in their school. Although many students may not have direct experience with migrating as depicted in *Siltent Dancing*, there may be those who have moved from one home or one school to another and can describe how it felt to be in a new physical and cultural environment. Students can record their responses either in a journal or through a graphic organizer. For an example, see Figure 2-1.

## Creating a Sense of Place

The stories in *Silent Dancing* paint strong images of people and the events that make up their lives. Equally powerful is the sense of place that is evoked through Cofer's use of descriptive language. Places and the objects in them provide very sensory images that live in our memories through sight, smell, sounds, touch, and sometimes even taste. Through language, the reader sees Mamá's house, which is "like a chambered nautilus" (p. 23), or the storytelling place of the mango tree with its thick leaves that "made a cool room" (p. 24). In "More Room," Cofer describes Mamá's bedroom and the pieces of furniture and objects in it. As you read this chapter, take a kind of mental virtual tour of the room and conjure up a picture of each object. Does the four-poster bed shine with a patina brought on with years of polishing fine wood? Can you smell the herbs that fill those jars on the dresser? How does the middle of Mamá's mattress feel as you snuggle in its safety? Creating a sense of place or setting is important to a good story and can make readers feel as though they are actually in the story with the rest of the characters. The following activities are some that I have used in my own writing as well as in teaching others how to develop a sense of place.

## Drawing a Site Map

If you close your eyes, you can probably call up a place that is

La Escuela Segundo Ruiz Belvis

*Physical description:*
Airy tropical architecture of yellow cement with
green trim (p. 51)

*Social/Cultural Issues:*
Twelve years of English instruction required
Previously content was taught in English only as part
of Americanization plan for the newly acquired
territory (p. 54)

P.S. 11

*Physical description:*
Functional and prison-like four-
storied red-brick with black steel fire
escapes; concrete playground
enclosed by chain-link fence (p. 65)

*Social/Cultural Issues:*
English only is language of
instruction; no bilingual or ESOL
instruction—immersion in English
(p. 65–66)

### Place: School

Name of your school

*Physical description:*
What is the outer appearance of your school?
What are the colors, construction materials,
other architectural features? How does this
compare with either school described in the text?

*Social/Cultural Issues:*
What are the language policies and programs in
your school? How do they compare with those
described in the text? How do you feel about
these issues?

**Figure 2-1.** Tracing New Environments

part of your everyday life. It could be your own room, your family's kitchen, or your neighbor's back yard. Can you visualize this place? What are the main features, like size and shape? What are some of the objects found here? For the following activities, it is a good idea to find a place that you and your class can visit at least a couple of times. Sometimes, I have students pick a place in the school building—the library, cafeteria, reading corner in the classroom, playground—to ensure easy and multiple access. Ethnographers often begin to get to know a place by drawing a *site map*. A site map is a representation of the physical location of where ethnographers study the human phenomena that are taking place. The site map is not an artistic drawing, but rather a rough sketch that identifies the important aspects of the site, such as its basic shape and dimensions, and the objects in it. Within the overall representational shape, draw boxes and write in each box a description that tells what the object is. For example, here is a site map of a classroom. See Figure 2-2.

After students draw their site maps at school, they should try drawing one of a place that is important in their lives outside of school.

## Taking Observational Field Notes

Another tool of the ethnographic researcher involves taking observational field notes. The term is fairly self-explanatory: You go to the physical site—researchers sometimes call this the field—where your study is taking place, and you write down what you observe or see. The important point to remember is that in writing down what you observe, you do not include language that may add an interpretive or subjective element to the description. This is a fairly straightforward description that records some of the physical properties and contents of a room. Try taking observational notes on a small area first, like your desk. Describe your desk and its contents, taking care not to include subjective descriptors like orderly, messy, disorganized, boring, and so on. For example, here is a description of my desk:

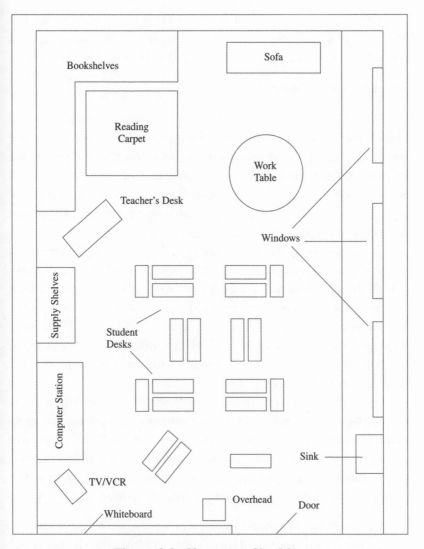

**Figure 2-2.** Classroom Site Map

The desk, made of a gray plastic laminate, is approximately 3 × 4 feet, and has one center drawer. On top of the desk, just over the center drawer, is a laptop computer. In the upper right-hand corner is a phone. A notepad and a dictionary are to the left of the computer.

After you have practiced and feel fairly comfortable with the process, go back to the place where you created your site map and record observational notes describing the site and the objects in it.

## The Dramatic Turn

Now that you have described the physical attributes of the place and its objects from the perspective of an ethnographic researcher taking field notes, take another look at the place and its objects from a different perspective, in a different role, which is more like a creative writer. I sometimes refer to this as the *dramatic turn*, which simply means adding descriptive language, based on your thoughts and feelings about the space, through use of action words and sensory images. Cofer skillfully creates a sense of place through imagery and action words in the chapter "More Room." Instead of a bedroom with a bed in it, she sees a "queen's room" that is "dominated" by the "massive four-poster bed in its center which stood taller than a child's head." You may want to reread this chapter, and, either individually or as a class, generate a list of similar examples. Continue adding to this list throughout your reading of the book.

Looking at your own field notes, begin your dramatic turn by adding descriptors based on sensory images and giving action to ordinary objects. You might start with the practice notes you recorded describing your desk. After you have brainstormed some words and phrases, write a few sentences that express the essence of your desk space. Here is what I did with my notes:

> The sparsely decorated desk gives off an air of togetherness, of orderliness, of organization. But, this is really smoke and mirrors. The "Silver Bullet," the titanium wonder that houses the random snippets of thoughts, scattered in mysterious acronym-labeled files on its cluttered desktop, flawlessly executes the deception.

After practicing the steps in this process, students should now use the same process to create short descriptive vignettes that portray the spaces that are familiar and memorable in their own lives.

## Collecting and Telling Stories

In the chapter "Tales Told under the Mango Tree," the narrator retells the story of "María Sabida," the legendary folk heroine who is "wiser than any other woman on the Island of Puerto Rico" (p. 74). The character of María Sabida is Mamá's model for the "prevailing woman" who uses her intelligence to transform her thieving and murderous husband into a kind and honest man. Under the mango tree, listening to the *cuentos* spun by Mamá, Cofer began to feel the power of words and soon began to entertain herself by making up her own stories. Later in the same chapter, the author draws from her own experience to spin a new tale about María Sabida.

Like Cofer, I too have memories of stories being told around my grandmother's kitchen table—folktales, family histories, stories of maiden aunts, and ghost stories. There were humorous stories, like the one about my Uncle Bebe and his flight of fancy in a glider that was built out of scrap lumber and propelled into the air with the aid of a Model A Ford, crashing seconds after liftoff. There were stories about historical disasters, like the one my grandmother told of her family's survival during Galveston's 1900 storm. These were some of the first stories that I collected and retold with my own twists and turns. As a child, I would keep mental files of all of the stories I heard around my grandmother's table, and as I grew older, I began keeping diaries of the family stories and stories I heard from friends. Along with my written retelling of the stories, I would keep a record of who told the stories and where they were told. Then, in a college history course, my instructor introduced me to the genre of oral history. My class project led me back to my grandmother and her own childhood memories of stories told about Galveston's infamous 1900 storm, which destroyed the island and took thousands of lives. After that class, my collection and documentation of stories began to take on a new dimension. I began to record not only the stories and short biographical notes about the tellers, but also began researching any historical events that were either embedded in the story itself or were contemporary with the storyteller and the story. Probably everyone can recall stories that have been told by a storyteller who is a family member, friend or even a teacher. Remembering a story may take a bit of coaxing out from years of filing away and may require travel back into childhood memory. Or, a good story may be one you heard just yesterday. Whatever the case, begin your own story collection by developing an annotated list, giving the story a title, then writing a brief summary of what the story is about. This list can provide you with a repertoire of stories that you can develop for performance. Stories can be collected by individuals, which usually works for older students, or the collection can be a class project in which stories about events and people in the class are developed. For example, in a classroom collection, there may be stories about field trips, interesting school assemblies, famous people who have come to the school, humorous happenings in class, individuals' stories, and so forth. Regardless of which direction you choose, the goal is to collect stories for performance.

## Telling a Story

What does it mean to tell a story? Storytelling is a person-to-person oral presentation of a narrative to an audience. A key ingredient in storytelling is the interaction created between the teller and the listener. This live circuit depends on both the teller and the listener being active and responsive to one another. The interplay generally results in the listener's nonverbal reactions to the story and the teller, and the teller's response to these communications through spontaneous improvisations that can alter intonation, adjust the pace, or even change the wording. Think about a comedy routine you have seen on television or heard in a live performance. How effective or enjoyable would the routine have been if the performer had not waited for the audience to laugh at the punch line? And, have you ever noticed how often the comedian speaks directly to an individual or asks rhetorical questions of audience members as a way of including them in the perform- ance? Storytellers use the same techniques to engage the audience in the performance. As a performance art, storytelling incorpo- rates gestures, facial expressions, and different vocal tones to cre- ate dramatic effects. In addition to using these performance tech- niques, an effective telling will also have well-developed literary elements, much like any well-written story. A strong story line that maintains a sequence of events leading to the "climax" or point of the story is one important feature of a good telling. This does not necessarily mean that the events have to be in chronological order. In fact, many good stories are told in a series of events that take place in the present mixed with flashbacks to the past. The char- acters should be portrayed with enough detail so that the listener can get a clear picture of the roles they play in the events and out- come of the story. And, a good telling combines imagery and descriptive language, a variety of sentence structures—questions, statements, dramatic exclamations—and use of dialogue to create interest. These elements of a good "telling" can be found in the story of "María Sabida." As students read the story, ask them to find examples of these elements and either record them in a response journal or highlight them in the text.

## Developing the Storytelling Process

Now that you are familiar with some examples of good story- telling elements, you can try your hand at developing one of your own stories. Choose one of the stories from your annotated list. Begin your story by creating a storymap. For example, in my story about my uncle's glider, the storymap sequence of events looks like this: See Figure 2-3.

Using your storymap as a guide, practice telling the story. Try telling a "draft" of your story using a tape recorder. Then, listen to the recording and make any necessary revisions. Here are some questions to help you in your revision:

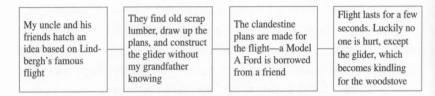

| My uncle and his friends hatch an idea based on Lindbergh's famous flight | They find old scrap lumber, draw up the plans, and construct the glider without my grandfather knowing | The clandestine plans are made for the flight—a Model A Ford is borrowed from a friend | Flight lasts for a few seconds. Luckily no one is hurt, except the glider, which becomes kindling for the woodstove |

**Figure 2-3.** Storymap/Sequence of Events

- Did you include a variety of sentence types?
- Do you need to add more descriptive language to create "rounder" or more developed characters?
- Does dialogue occur between characters?
- Have you included all the important events in the story's sequence?

After you have revised your story, practice again with the revisions and try performing it in front of a small audience—such as a good friend or family members. Remember to include the different storytelling techniques that will engage your listeners—different intonation in dialogue sequences and, for dramatic effect, appropriate gestures and facial expressions. Remember to respond to your audience's nonverbal signals—adjust the pace, insert a rhetorical question here, change a word or two there. This is probably the most difficult part of becoming a good storyteller. The key is to keep telling the story, and telling it to different audiences. This repetition will help you revise and refine the story's content as well as the performance. Like Cofer, you can also create a written version of the story. Just make sure that you write down what you actually tell. This will keep the essence of orality, which is the key ingredient in storytelling, in your written work.

## Researching the Story

What is the history of your story? Where did you first hear it told? Who told it? Is it an old family story or is it a folktale that has been handed down? To find these answers, go back to the source of the story, the storyteller. If access to the original storyteller is not possible, you might talk to someone who is also familiar with the story, such as a family member or friend. One important research tool I learned to use when I began gathering oral histories was the *ethnographic interview*. An ethnographic interview uses open-ended questions to allow the person being interviewed a less structured format for responding. Planning and writing some open-ended interview questions will help you to get the information needed to build the background history of the story. It is important to remember that a good interview question is one that cannot be answered with a simple yes or no. Questions, allowing the interviewee latitude in her or his answers, usually begin with, "Can you describe?" or "Tell me about..." Another important technique for interviewing is to cluster the questions around similar topics so that the interview can follow a natural flow of talk. Here are some examples of topics and questions to help you get started. I am sure you can think of many more. Remember, the content of the story will naturally shape the kinds of questions you will ask. In other words, if the story is a folktale, you will not have to ask if the story is based on a personal experience.

- *Topic:* Storyteller's background
  *Questions:* Can you tell me a little about yourself? Can you describe how you got started telling stories? What other stories do you tell?
- *Topic:* History of the story
  *Questions:* Can you describe the origins of the story? Who told the story first? What do you know about this person?
- *Topic:* Setting or occasion
  *Questions:* When and where was the story typically told—on certain holidays, at family gatherings, around the campfire?

When you are conducting the interview, the person you are interviewing may introduce some information that may require more explanation. A good interviewer will depart from the "script" of questions and ask for more detail with a question like, "Can you tell me more about that?" This kind of flexibility comes with practice, so, at first, you might want to stick with your original questions without deviation. Another strategy that is often used by good interviewers occurs when the person being interviewed strays from the topic. A good way to bring the interview back on track is to say something like, "Getting back to the question . . ." Researchers tape record their interviews so they will have an accurate record of the information being discussed. Tape recording allows the interviewer to concentrate on the interview and the person being interviewed without having to write down extensive notes and verbatim quotes, which can often be a distraction and can disrupt the flow. However, always be sure to ask permission before you do any tape recording.

Using the responses from the interview, you can write up the information in different genre forms. For example, one format is a transcription of the interview. To do this, you need to listen to the tape recording and write down exactly what was said. In other words, what you will generate is a verbatim text. A typical format looks like this excerpt from an interview with my grandmother when I was researching her story of Galveston's 1900 storm.

Joan:    *Can you describe the setting or what occasion you first heard the story based on your family's experience in the storm?*

Rosalee:  I can't remember exactly when the first time was, but we always heard the story during hurricane season, especially when a hurricane was heading for Galveston. I don't really remember being in the storm myself, I was only a baby. But, I can tell you every detail because I heard it so many times.

Since this process is time-consuming, use of a word-processor is recommended. Another helpful hint is to listen to the interview first and locate instances in the interview that are particularly rich in information, noting the counter number so that you can concentrate on that portion in your transcribing.

Another way to present the information from the interview is to write a biographical sketch about the storyteller that includes the history or other information gained about the story. A sketch, unlike a full biography, is a short essay that outlines those important details that are relevant to the part of the person's life being highlighted. In this case, your sketch will include those details that are related to the person as a storyteller and the story. But, you do not have to be limited to these more traditional representations of informational data. You can interpret the storyteller through poetry. A simple formula poem is the *biopoem*. There are different versions of the formula that vary the line length and number of descriptors. Here is the eight-line version:

Line 1:     First name of the person
Line 2:     Two adjectives describing the person
Line 3:     Sibling or relative of . . .
Line 4:     Lover of . . . (name two things)
Line 5:     Who fears . . . (name two things)
Line 6:     Who would like to see…(name two things)
Line 7:     Resident of . . . (the city in which the person lives)
Line 8:     Last name

Any of these forms, the interview, the biographical sketch, the poem, can be used as an introduction to the oral performance of the story or as a preface to the story's written version. For example, try performing some excerpts from the interview transcription as a reading for two voices. For a multimedia effect, play a portion of the interview tape (remember to ask permission). Mix it up and try different combinations. The point is to keep your story alive and fresh for the audience's enjoyment, but also for your own.

## Most Memorable Persons

As Cofer demonstrates, personal memoir is much more than writing about the events of your life. Personal memoir encompasses the people whose stories intertwine with yours, people who leave their imprint of influence on you, people who help to shape your identity. There are many such memorable people in *Silent Dancing*. There is Mamá, whose voice first influences the writer's own. But, there are others who have also contributed to the author's identity. As you read about these people, here are some questions to guide the discussions about the role each character plays in the life of the author.

- Why did the author include this person's story?
- What influence did this person have on the author's life?
- Is there someone whom you know that has a similar story to one of the characters in *Silent Dancing*? How is the story similar?
- How has this person influenced your life?

After the discussion, write a vignette—a short narrative— either about a person from the story or about a memorable person in your life.

## Working with Words

The author of *Silent Dancing* uses many Spanish words in her writing. Her careful placement of these words within the natural flow of the sentence adds richness and a cultural flavor to the stories. The technique of embedding the definition of the word within the text provides the reader with the meaning without having to look up the word in a dictionary. Each Spanish word is also italicized for easy identification. For example, on page 15, the definition of the Spanish word *cuentos* is described in the adjacent text as "morality and cautionary tales." The author continues to build the meaning of the word for the reader by expanding the definition to include the ways the *cuentos* influenced her life. This added dimension of personal meaning attached to the word by the author gives the reader even more insight into the deeper structure of the word. Using the strategy of gaining the meaning of words through surrounding context is a good one to practice for the non-Spanish and Spanish speaker alike. To develop this strategy, and at the same time build vocabulary, create a bilingual dictionary by listing the words and their meanings in an individual vocabulary journal or class dictionary. Remember to record the page number on which the word and definition are located for easy reference in literature circle or class discussions. Talking about new vocabulary and how context clues are used to help construct their meaning should become a regular part of discussions about the book. One way to organize your dictionary/journal is to divide the page into the following columns:

| Page # | Word | Contextual Definition |
|--------|------|----------------------|
| 15 | *cuentos* | morality and cautionary tales |
| 30 | *pruebas* | tests of one's abilities |

These examples are fairly easy to identify in the text. However, there are some that are more challenging. For example, can you determine the meaning of the word *prometida* from the passage beginning with the third paragraph on page 71? What do you think the difference is between *prometida* and *prometido*? What are the context clues that lead you to your conclusions?

After we learn new vocabulary words, we begin to make them our own by using them in ways that are specific to our lives. The author provides not only the definition to the words in the surrounding context, she also uses the words in ways that further extend the meaning as it fits within the story. Take, for example, the word *cuentos*. We know these are "morality and cautionary tales" from the adjacent context. However, the author gives us additional clues about the *cuentos* that are specific to her life. They were "told by women in my family for generations" and they "became a part of my subconscious." These additional clues extend the meaning of the word such that it reaches past the surface meaning of tales or stories. In the author's further explanation, *cuentos* spring from an oral tradition in which women are the primary storytellers, and these stories are an integral part of who the author is as a person. You may want to add a fourth column titled **Author's Extended Meaning**. In this column, write the phrases or sentences that illustrate the author's specific meaning attached to the word. Discussion of the ways the author further extends the meanings of words can become the main focus for students who are Spanish speakers. In addition, these students can discuss the specific ways these words are used in their own families and individual experiences.

If you want to build dictionary skills along with using context clues for meanings of words, include the task of looking up the word in a Spanish/English dictionary. You can record the definition in another column titled **Dictionary Meaning**.

## Connecting across the Curriculum

Columbus's landing on the island of Borinquen in 1493 precipitated a chain of events that dramatically changed the course of the world's history and had far-reaching effects on the island and people of Puerto Rico. One way to extend the discussions generated through reading *Silent Dancing* into other content areas is through a thematic project approach in which students create various museum exhibits. Through performance of such authentic tasks as museum archivists and curators, students can learn about the different aspects of Puerto Rico, past and present, in content areas such as anthropology, history, political science, and the arts. Museum archivists and curators generally oversee the cataloguing and exhibition of museum collections. Their jobs include researching and writing about the historical and other background information of the collection. They may also organize and coordinate the educational programs that accompany these collections. While these general duties are similar for both archivist and curator, there are differences in the artifacts that each handles. Archivists deal with documents and records, such as photographs, letters, and books. Curators generally handle objects, such as paintings, sculpture, and textiles. In the following activities, students can develop their researching, reading, writing, organizational, and presentation strategies. The project can also provide an educational experience for other students, parents, and the community.

If there is a museum in your city, you might invite one of the curators or archivists to your class to explain what it is he does. Or, if possible, visit the museum and see these people in their natural workplace. At the same time, students can see the various kinds of exhibits—paintings, books, statues, maps, pottery, clothing—and get ideas of how exhibits are displayed. If you cannot travel to a museum, the Metropolitan Museum of Art or the Museum of Modern Art in New York City can be accessed online. This virtual visit can stimulate interest and provide a background for the class museum project.

## The History and Culture of the Taínos

Part of Puerto Rico's rich cultural heritage stems from the early inhabitants of the island—the Taínos. To build a greater understanding of these historical roots, students can assemble a museum exhibit presenting information about the Taíno people. For this exhibit, since the information gathered will most likely be in the form of illustrations, maps, information from secondary sources such as journals or diaries, or modern accounts of history found in texts and media, students will act as archivists for the exhibit. Divide the class into teams of archivists. Assign each team to research and collect artifacts. Research areas can be designated by broad categories such as: (a) *Habitat*—geographical features, (b) *Social Structure*—family units, governing, trade/economic resources, (c) *Arts*, and, (d) *Encounter*—the decline and fall after Columbus's landing. After the research areas are defined and assigned to teams, begin the research. A Web search can provide some sites that give an overview of Taíno history and culture. There are also some texts that are excellent resources. *The Taínos: Rise and Decline of the People Who Greeted Columbus,* by noted anthropologist Irving Rouse, is a complete and well-documented account of Taíno history. The information gathered in the various research areas will determine the kinds of artifacts that are collected. For example, the collection may include primary source materials, such as diary excerpts from the logs of Christopher Columbus. There could also be drawings of maps of Caribbean islands, and the northern part of South America to illustrate the areas where the Taínos migrated.

The next step is to assemble the artifacts and write exhibit labels for each. An exhibit label generally lists the name of the artifact and then supplies a brief explanation or description. For example, students may draw a map of the West Indies to illustrate the geographical relationship of the islands to each other within this large designation. The label might look something like this:

---

**A Map of the West Indies**

The island chain of the West Indies can be divided into three groups: the Lesser Antilles, the Greater Antilles, and the Bahamian Archipelago. Within each of these are smaller clusters of islands. Puerto Rico, Cuba, Hispaniola, and Jamaica form the Greater Antilles group.

---

**Figure 2-4.** Museum Placard

## Music Traditions

The influence of the Spanish, Taíno, and African cultures can be heard in the music being played and danced to in Puerto Rico today. During the Spanish colonial period, many musical traditions developed that had roots in the folk songs and ballads of eighteenth- and nineteenth-century Spain. *Jíbaro* folk music originated in the Andalusian (southern) region of Spain. With the arrival of African slaves during the colonial period came the influence of African musical traditions. One distinctly African dance form is the *bomba*. Many of the musical forms heard in Puerto Rico today, such as the *plena*, represent a fusion of African call and response structures and rhythms fused with Spanish melodies.

In addition to traditional Western instruments, such as modern stringed instruments (violin, cello), brass (trumpet, saxophone, trombone), and the piano, there are a number of musical instruments with roots in the Spanish, Taíno, and African cultures. When the Spanish colonized the Caribbean islands, they brought their music. The primary instrument was the Spanish guitar. Similar guitar-like instruments with roots in Spain were the *requinto,* the *bordonúa,* and the *cuatro,* which is unique to Puerto Rico. You may recall that the *cuatro* is one of the instruments played in the tale of "María Sabida." Also mentioned in the story are the *güiro* and the *maracas.* The *güiro,* a type of percussion instrument made from a hollowed-out gourd, originated with the Taínos. The *maracas,* also a percussion instrument made from gourds filled with pebbles or dried beans, may have African and/or indigenous roots.

As archivists, students can research the history of various musical forms, such as the *décima, seis, habanera, aguinaldo, plena, bomba,* and *salsa.* As part of the exhibit, collect recordings of the various examples of the musical forms being played today. There are a number of artists recording in different musical genres. Exhibit these artifacts along with the written description of the type of musical form, and set up a tape recorder with headphones, one for each example, so the museum visitor can listen to an example of each form. If you have access to digital equipment (computer with CD-ROM), the written description can be linked to the audio example, providing a computer-based interactive component. As curators, students can research and assemble different instruments that produce the various musical forms. Just like the artifacts in the Taíno exhibit, create a label for each instrument.

## The United States and Puerto Rico: Politics Past and Present

As a result of the Spanish-American War, the United States and Puerto Rico became tied together in a political, economic, and cultural relationship that continues today. Students can research and collect important historic documents that reflect political policy, government legislation, and judicial decisions, such as the *Foraker Act* and the *Jones Act,* the court case of *Downs vs. Biddell,* the election of Puerto Rico's first native governor, Luis Muñoz Marín, and the economic program called *Operation Bootstrap*. In the present political scene, the debates concerning the relationship of the United States and Puerto Rico center on becoming a state, continuing as a commonwealth, or moving toward independence. Students can research what it means to be a commonwealth of the United States. Who exactly governs Puerto Rico? Are the civil rights of the citizens of Puerto Rico the same as those of U.S.-born citizens? How would a change to statehood affect the island's citizens, government, and economy? These and other questions can form the basis of a debate students can present as part of an *educational lecture series* accompanying the exhibits in the class museum.

## Exhibiting and Presenting What You Learned

Now that you have all the exhibits ready to display, you can turn your classroom, or larger space such as a gym or cafeteria, into a museum. The project fits well into a schoolwide event such as an open house, parents' night, or other community function. This is an opportunity for students to present their work through the exhibits and also make presentations about their work. As part of the lecture series, in addition to the political debate, the program can include poetry readings taken from *Silent Dancing* or other collections by Cofer, as well from other notable Puerto Rican poets, such as Luis Palés Matos. The series can also include storytelling. Students can present their own stories developed in the Response section of this chapter, or other Puerto Rican folktales or myths they have read. Another way students can present what they learned is through the role of museum docent. As docents, students act as guides through the various exhibits. Docents also present narrated speeches that give the visitors information about the exhibit and artifacts in it.

The museum project provides students with opportunities to develop different learning strategies that involve researching, reading, writing, speaking, listening, organizing, and performing what they have learned in an authentic way. What is equally important, however, is the sharing of this learning with other students, parents, and community members in such a way that everyone involved in the project benefits from this multidimensional learning experience centered in the rich cultural heritage of the people of Puerto Rico.

## Summary

The stories in *Silent Dancing: A Partial Remembrance of a Puerto Rican Childhood* present vivid memories of people, places, events, and retold tales that are a part of the author's life. In the Preface to the book, Cofer refers to the difficulty of writing about one's own life. Drawing on Virginia Woolf's explanation that such writing is a combination of memory and imagination, Cofer writes her *ensayos*. This Spanish word for essays, which also means a rehearsal or practice, suggests a moment that is not the actual event, but a version of that event based on both memory and imagination. Cofer describes this kind of writing as "creative nonfiction," which is a combination of fiction and nonfiction. While the event or the person may be based on fact, the writer creates a holistic image, much like the poet, through manipulation of descriptive language to create a version of the "truth." Thus, through the power of words, we can reclaim memories and lessons from the past and transform them into stories that help us discover meaning in the present. This is the unifying theme of Cofer's *ensayos,* and through them, we, as readers and writers, can also discover the transformative power of language.

# Chapter 3

# *Call Me Consuelo:*
# Mystery and Subplot

## Story Summary

The novel *Call Me Consuelo* contains two plots, a main plot and a subplot. The main plot is a mystery with a crime to be solved. The subplot traces a young girl's adjustment to living in a new place that is very different both culturally and geographically from her old home. These two intertwining plots begin when Maria Consuelo Harburton has to move to Los Angeles to live with her grandmother, Grace. Consuelo, as she likes to be called, had been living with her aunt and uncle since her parents died in a car accident. When Tío Fernando loses his job, Consuelo's grandmother decides that she belongs with her. In her new home, not only must she cope with a new life away from her Tía Alma and Tío Fernando and all of her cousins in the little mining town of Dos Palos, but she is also thrown into a dangerous mystery that she is determined to solve.

The story begins with Consuelo's arrival at Shadywood Knolls, a security-gated community that has been built on the site of an old movie lot. In fact, some of the lot is still standing behind a tall fence at the back of the complex. When Consuelo climbs a tree to get a better view, she sees the remains of some of the old sets. There is the New York street scene with building facades representing a newspaper office, the *New York Gazette*. There is also a castle, complete with a drawbridge. But, the best on the lot is the old fort that has a real tower. Consuelo is determined to find a way over the high fence so she can see the lot up close.

Meanwhile, at school, Consuelo is making new friends. Lish, whose name is really Alicia, also lives in Shadywood Knolls. Besides helping Consuelo find her way around at school, she also helps her find Rusty Neeland's house, also in Shadywood Knolls. Consuelo's teacher has asked her to drop some papers by for Rusty, who is home with a broken leg. Actually, he broke his leg in an attempt to get over the fence and onto the old movie lot to retrieve the cameras he had lost on an earlier visit. After hearing about the lot and the missing cameras from Rusty, Consuelo makes up her mind to climb the tree by Rusty's back wall and drop over the fence. She convinces her new friend, Lish, to accompany her.

As Lish and Consuelo are exploring the lot, they discover some interesting things. The set is mostly just facades—storefronts without any sides or back. But, the fort is a three-sided structure. And, the tower is real. While looking for the cameras in the fort, Consuelo discovers some orange peels that are scattered all around a box full of oranges. Either someone else is here, or had been at one time. Both girls get this creepy feeling that someone is watching them. Suddenly, when they hear a scream, they run to get back over the fence. With some effort they finally find some loose boards in the fence and cross back to the safety of Shadywood Knolls, but not before marking the place on the fence boards where they can get back in.

When Consuelo finds that she has apparently lost her locket that has her parents' pictures in it at the movie lot, she determines she must go back for it. The next day at school, Rusty tells her about the mysterious light he saw in one of the lower rooms of the fort the night before. They begin to put together the clues they have so far—the orange peels, the scream, the light, and the missing cameras. Also, there have been recent burglaries in the Shadywood Knolls complex. Can all of this be related somehow? Whatever the case, no matter the danger, Consuelo has to go back to the movie lot and retrieve her locket. That is when she meets Ellen Marie, who is also at the lot looking for her bookbag she had left there the day before.

Now, Ellen Marie is in trouble. She has twisted her ankle on the old, rickety boardwalk lining the storefronts, and can't walk. To make matters worse, Ellen tells Consuelo she has seen two men in the fort. When they hear heavy footsteps in the tower, they decide to make a run for it and luckily escape without being detected. Consuelo is sure there is something very suspicious going on at the movie lot, and at school the next day, she and her friends make a plan to return to the movie lot on Saturday. On her way home from school, Consuelo discovers that there have been more robberies, and this time, her home has also been robbed.

Saturday arrives, and Lish, Domingo, and Consuelo, armed with streamers that Rusty has given them to throw over the fence as a signal they are in danger, enter the lot. Once in, Consuelo again meets Ellen, who came on her own to get her bookbag. In the end, what they find is much more than cameras and a bookbag. In the tower, Consuelo and her friends find TVs, VCRs, computers, a fur coat, silverware, and other valuable items. What they have discovered is the hiding place for all the stolen goods from the Shadywood Knoll robberies. They are about to make a run for it to get help, when the burglars arrive. Consuelo knows their only hope is to get outside and throw the streamers so Rusty will know they are in trouble. Seeing the streamers, Rusty tells his dad, who calls the police. The burglars are arrested before any harm comes to the group.

Everything seems to be getting back to normal in Shadywood Knolls. There is just one question left unanswered. How did the burglars get in and out of the security-gated community so often and so easily? Piecing together clues, Consuelo and her friends remember that they overheard the burglars talking about another person they called Chezz, who wasn't there when the arrests took place. Who could this Chezz person be? It turns out that Chezz is really Mr. Chester Crane, called Chezz by everyone in the complex. He is also arrested as an accomplice in the burglaries.

At the end of the story, Consuelo receives two letters. One is from her cousin Rebecca, the other from Tío Fernando. Both tell her that she will be able to return to Dos Palos soon. Finally, it seems that what she has been hoping for is about to come true. She should be as "happy as Christmas." But, Consuelo isn't. What she really wants to do is to stay with her grandmother. It seems that living with Grace and all of her new and sometimes kooky friends is "a very eclectic thing to do."

## Building Background Before You Read

Ofelia Dumas Lachtman was born in Los Angeles, California, which is also the setting for *Call Me Consuelo*. Her parents were both born in Mexico, and Lachtman grew up speaking both Spanish and English, much like the heroine of the story. Lachtman's stories contain themes that are closely related to her own life, particularly the importance of maintaining one's bilingual and bicultural identity. In *Call Me Consuelo*, the main character experiences the tension between wanting to establish new friendships and a relationship with her grandmother in an English-only environment and needing to maintain her sense of self that is tied to her Spanish-speaking family and community that she is forced to leave. Consuelo's story is similar to many real-life stories of people living in the United States who are faced with the dilemma of surviving a new culture while trying to maintain their own heritage culture and language.

The connections between language and culture and their influences on how we define who we are, how we frame our thoughts and construct our worldviews are an implicit but strong theme underlying this story. The interconnectedness of culture, identity, and language is also the subject of many theories and ongoing debates in various linguistic, educational, sociological, and political arenas in our country today. While it is beyond the scope and purpose of this chapter to explore these theories or debates fully, we can take a brief look at some of the historical factors that have contributed to some of these discussions.

### Immigration, Acculturation, Americanization

Although English has never been officially mandated as the language of the United States, a prevalent assumption held by many Americans and promoted by the social, political, and economic institutions in our country is that English is *the* language of currency and the dominant language of instruction in educational institutions. English as the predominant institutionalized language of the United States has its historical roots in British colonization because many of the first colonists came from Great Britain. However, there were a number of languages other than English spoken in colonial America. In addition to the indigenous languages other than English spoken by people from the various Native American Indian nations, there were also languages spoken by immigrants from countries other than Great Britain, such as German, a predominant language spoken in Pennsylvania. Although there was a proliferation of languages in use other than English in colonial times, there were often debates concerning the use of a language other than English, particularly in the public arena. It has been reported that Benjamin Franklin expressed concern over the alleged refusal by Pennsylvania Germans to speak English and their insistence on the use of bilingual street signs. While intolerance toward non-English language use existed, a more common attitude was the promotion of voluntary assimilation through bilingualism (Crawford, 1992). However, rather than a real advocacy for bilingualism, this stance may have been prompted by a recognition of the need to translate key documents related to the Revolution, in order to persuade colonists who spoke languages other than English (primarily French and German) to join the revolutionary cause (Heath, as cited in Crawford, 1992).

Intolerance of language use other than English was explicitly practiced toward conquered and colonized peoples from colonial times and well after the establishment of the United States. Indigenous Native American peoples and Spanish-speaking residents of territories in the South, Southwest, and Puerto Rico, which were ceded to the United States after wars with Mexico and Spain, were subjected to Americanization policies that promoted acculturation through instruction in a unifying English-only system. Many Native American children were removed from their homes and sent to boarding schools where English was the language of instruction, and children were punished if caught speaking their first language. In the Southwest, the 1848 Treaty of Guadalupe Hidalgo, which formally ended the Mexican-American War, granted citizenship to all Mexican nationals who wanted to remain in the ceded territory of California, Texas, Arizona, and New Mexico. The treaty ensured various civil, political, and religious rights to the new Spanish-speaking citizens. Although language and cultural rights are not explicitly defined in the Treaty of Guadalupe Hidalgo, many believe that protection of the Spanish language and culture was an implicit intention of the treaty. According to Crawford (1992), the issue of language rights was seldom raised, except in the case of New Mexico, where language rights became part of the battle in the struggle for statehood. In New Mexico, Spanish speakers greatly outnumbered English speakers before the twentieth century. As a result, in 1912, when New Mexico was finally admitted, the state adopted a constitution that outlined certain protections for its Spanish-speaking citizens—in reality, all of the constitutions of these states were written in English and Spanish and laws were published in both languages. The intent of the Treaty of Guadalupe Hidalgo has been part of many recent debates concerning English-only and bilingualism issues that have affected language instruction policies in many of our schools here in the United States. In the case of Puerto Rico, as we learned in *Silent Dancing*, English as the language of instruction in schools was part of the Americanization of the island during the time of Cofer's parents' education. By the time Cofer attended school on the island, instruction was in Spanish, with English taught as a second language.

Regardless of the time period or the predominant stance toward English language usage and Americanization, it is probably safe to say that from the founding of this country, language has played a prominent role in the history of the United States. Often the issue of language use has been associated with nationalism. Speaking standard American English (as opposed to British

English) became an activity linked with patriotism. Because of this, language has been a primary target of the Americanization policies toward indigenous peoples and non-English-speaking people immigrating to the United States. Many of these attitudes and policies continue today. Since many children in our classrooms today come from diverse linguistic and cultural backgrounds, it is important for teachers to recognize the necessity of becoming literate in English in a society that privileges English as the currency of access. However, equally important is the recognition of the effects that acculturation and Americanization can have on a person's sense of self and his or her relationships with family and cultural and linguistic heritage. Moreover, in a shrinking multicultural world, speaking more than one language—especially a world language like Spanish—is an economic, educational, and diplomatic asset.

In the poem "Elena," Pat Mora paints a poignant portrait of a Spanish-speaking mother who experiences the distancing of her children as they learn to speak English. Such linguistic distancing not only affects the everyday communication between family members, it can also be devastating to the passing down of a cultural and historical heritage through narrative tradition. This is a reality for many children in our schools today, who suddenly find themselves between two cultures, having to re-identify themselves, while coping with difficulties in communicating and living in both worlds. While the main character in *Call Me Consuelo* is bilingual in Spanish and English, she, like many students in our classrooms today, is faced with loneliness for her culturally familiar surroundings and the loss of being able to communicate in her first language.

As you prepare to read *Call Me Consuelo,* ask students to think of the different places and the language used in each context that are part of their everyday lives. Linguists often refer to these as domains of use. These spaces of experience and communication are integral parts of our everyday lives in which we participate and use language. Within a space there can be a number of contexts where different kinds of language are used. For example, in

school, there is a specific kind of language required for participation in the classroom, and this is sometimes very different from
the language used on the playground or cafeteria. Language use
in school spaces may also differ from home spaces. Knowing how
and when to use different forms of language or discourses is
referred to as communicative competence (Hymes, 1977).

The language used in these spaces of experience and communication may also be linguistically different. To prepare students to think about issues of language use and how these may
affect students whose first language is one other than English, ask
them to think about these questions. Do you speak another language other than English? Have you ever wanted to learn another language? Do students in your school speak only English in the
classroom and another language on the playground or in the
cafeteria? Why might this be important for them? What languages
do you or students that you know use outside of school? Would it
be appropriate for you or your friends to speak only English or
standard English (instead of a regional dialect) when communicating with grandparents or elders? Have you ever been in a space
where a language was being spoken that you did not understand?
How did this make you feel? These kinds of questions can open
up discussions about the connections between language and culture and how these influence one's sense of self and relationships
with family, friends, and community.

## Mystery as Genre Study

I often use genre studies as an effective way to build students'
understanding of the characteristics of different literary genre
and, at the same time, provide students with culturally diverse perspectives within those genre categories. As we have discussed previously, the underlying plot, or subplot of *Call Me Consuelo* gives the
reader insight into the cultural and linguistic issues that a young
girl faces when she is placed in an environment that is very different from the one she has known. The main plot that moves this
subplot along is a mystery, which is a type of realistic fiction that

contains elements of suspense. The story can be used as part of a genre study of realistic fiction that also provides a perspective on the importance of language and culture to one's identity.`

There is sometimes a feeling among teachers that mysteries are not as "literary" as realistic fiction, and therefore, they are often not included in instruction. However, mystery is one of the most popular types of realistic fiction among young adult readers. A mystery that contains the elements of realistic fiction—a good plot, believable and well-developed characters, realistic setting, and a theme that is not overly didactic—can be just as much a good piece of literature as any other well-crafted fiction novel.

When writing a mystery novel, the author employs some specific techniques that provide the element of suspense that sets mystery apart from other realistic fiction. First and probably foremost is the element of surprise. A good mystery takes readers on a roller-coaster ride of twists and turns, keeping them in a state of suspense and wondering what unexpected thing will happen next. A skillful mystery writer usually incorporates this into the first few pages. For example, in the first chapter of the novel, when Consuelo and her grandmother are driving into the Shadywood Knolls complex, Consuelo sees what appears to be a tower of a fort that was sitting just behind one of the buildings. This incongruity provides an element of surprise and also provides *foreshadowing* of the place that is the center of the mystery. The use of foreshadowing or providing a subtle glimpse of what is to come is another technique of the mystery writer. Questions that are left unanswered, at least for a short time, also help to build suspense. For example, in the first chapter of the novel, when Juan Pablo's whereabouts are discussed, it posed an unanswerable question that sets the tone for the possibility of a mysterious disappearance. This question also provides a background clue when suspicion is cast on Juan Pablo as the possible suspect for the thefts that are occurring at Shadywood Knolls. Also known as *red herrings*, casting suspicion on the wrong character is a great technique used to keep the reader guessing and make the mystery harder to solve. Finally, another important technique that builds suspense and creates a scary and sinister mood is the use of natural phenomena, such as thunderstorms or other severe weather conditions. Descriptive language that builds suspense and suggests a scary mood can also build tension. Think about the novels you have read that describe doorknobs turning noiselessly in a dark room, or shadows moving against the wall, or, as in this novel, a mysterious light late at night in the fort tower.

As you prepare to read *Call Me Consuelo,* ask students to think about what kinds of things make a novel a mystery. You can create a list of these responses and arrange them into categories that may be similar to the ones discussed above, such as:

- Element of surprise
- Foreshadowing
- Unanswered questions
- Red herrings
- Use of natural phenomena to create a mood
- Descriptive language that creates suspense

In the next section you will use these categories as you read the text. Learning to identify examples of these techniques can help students learn how to incorporate them into their own mystery writing.

### Reading and Responding to the Story

In the previous section, we discussed the different techniques that a mystery writer uses to create a suspenseful plot. In *Call Me Consuelo,* the author uses these techniques as she develops the *main plot,* which centers on mysterious goings-on at an old movie set. There is also another plot, a *subplot,* which deals with the main character's efforts to adapt to a new lifestyle. Both plots are carefully blended so that as readers continually discover more clues to the mystery, they are also learning more about the cultural differences Consuelo experiences as she adjusts to her new environment.

## Developing Higher-Order Thinking Skills

I am a great fan of mysteries and have read all kinds—detective novels, gothic novels, suspense thrillers, historical mysteries, even fantasy mysteries. The big attraction for me is trying to guess "who did it." This requires keeping track of all those clues that the author provides the reader and being wary of those blind alleys and red herrings that are put in one's path. It really gets the blood pumping if I can figure out the solution before anyone else. At the end of the book, if I am right in my guess, I feel pretty smug about outsmarting the detective hero or heroine. Being able to synthesize clues and formulate a hypothesis, or coming to a conclusion based on these clues, reflects use of higher-order thinking skills. The following activities focus on developing these skills through reading mystery plots. Building recognition of how a subplot develops and supports the main plot, as well as what techniques the author uses to build suspense, are also emphasized.

## Just Keep to the Facts, Ma'am

In many mysteries, the police detective who questions the witnesses about a crime records the *facts* that the witness remembers, usually in a little tablet that can fit easily into his or her pocket. These facts are the clues that detectives try to piece together to solve the mystery. As students read the novel, ask them to write down the clues they are given throughout the story. Providing a small wire-bound notepad adds to the overall effect. If you are reading the book in literature circles or as a class novel, ask students to discuss the clues they have collected after reading the passage on page 68 in the text. This is where Rusty says, "Let's put what we know together." As students contribute the clues they have recorded to this point, record them on an overhead and then ask students to hypothesize what might be going on in the fort, based on the clues that have been listed. Be sure to record the different hypotheses. After completing the book, you can refer back to the hypotheses to compare the actual conclusion with the students' predictions.

## Investigating the Subplot

In the novel, the author has created a subplot that tells the story of Consuelo's new life in Los Angeles with her Anglo grandmother, Grace. In this new environment, Consuelo has to adjust to doing things differently than in Dos Palos. In the first chapter, we discover that one of the first things she must cope with is not being able to speak Spanish with anyone. Coming from a home and community in which Spanish is spoken, she has a significant void in her life. It is important to note, however, that Consuelo is bilingual, because she attends an English-only school in Los Angeles and speaks English fluently. There are other cultural as well as social differences between her new life and the one she lived in Dos Palos. As students read the book and keep a record of the differences between her new environment in Los Angeles and the one she left behind in Dos Palos, also ask them to respond to how they think she feels about these differences. For example,

| Dos Palos | Los Angeles | Consuelo's response |
|---|---|---|
| Spanish is spoken in the home and community. | Her grandmother cannot speak Spanish; none of her new friends speaks Spanish. | She wishes she had someone to speak Spanish with, because it is part of who she is; it is a natural thing to do. |

**Figure 3-1.** Differences in Environments

## Searching for Mystery Techniques

Before you read the novel, you brainstormed a list of what kinds of things make a novel a mystery and organized these responses into categories—Elements of Surprise, Foreshadowing, Unanswered Questions, Red Herrings, Natural Phenomena, and Descriptive Language to Create Suspense. Using chart paper, cut in six-foot sections, write these categories as headings and tape them around the room. As students read the book, ask them to write a line of text or a summary that represents the technique that the author used. For example, in the first chapter, the question of what a fort was doing on Shadywood Knolls's property is an *unanswered question.* The answer, that Shadywood Knolls is built on an old movie lot, comes in Chapter 3, and also provides an element of surprise.

## Writing a Mystery Story

After reading and responding to the novel, students can try their hand at writing a mystery story. Begin by using the examples that the students wrote in the previous activity to review the different techniques that an author uses to create suspense in a mystery plot. Discussing their responses will provide concrete examples for their own writing. The next step is a prewriting activity. Collect newspaper articles that report burglaries. These real-life situations often provide starting points for a good mystery story. Students then choose and read the article. As they read, they should record the important facts reported about the burglary, much in the same way they did in the earlier clue-collecting activity. Next, students should pose some questions that appear to be unanswered in the article. For example: Why did the burglars choose that particular place? What were they looking for? Could it have been an "inside job?" These provide some of the unanswered questions that they may want to use as a suspense-building technique in their stories. The answers can be developed as clues that readers learn throughout the story that will eventually lead to solving the crime.

Once students have an idea for their mystery, they can begin to think about the different elements that make up the story. Begin by creating the *main character.* Will the character be a girl or a boy? What does the character look like? Does she have curly hair? Is he tall? Where does the person go to school? What kinds of things does he or she do at home and at school? What are the character's strengths and weaknesses? For example, does the character always tell the truth? Does he or she make friends easily? Semantic webbing is a good tool to use in developing the character's traits.

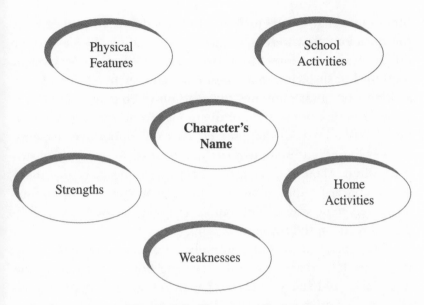

**Figure 3-2.** Character Traits

After a main character is in place, create some minor characters for the story. A minor character could be like Lish in the novel, a friend who helps solve the mystery. It is always good to have a friend for the main character to talk to in order to sort the clues. There can also be minor characters who are not so friendly and get in the way of solving the crime, like Mr. Crane, who turned out to be a villain.

Now that you have your idea and characters, decide how your story is going to end. In other words, how will the mystery be solved? Will the main character set a trap for the burglars and catch them red-handed? Or, will the main character get caught sleuthing and have to escape and get help? Once you have decided how the story will end and the mystery is solved, think of a crucial clue that is the one that provides the information to help the main character solve the crime. For example, the crucial clue in *Call Me Consuelo* is when the stolen goods from Shadywood Knolls are found in the fort.

After developing your crucial clue, you should make a list of other clues that will be included in the story. Remember to use the questions that were generated after reading the newspaper article. And, don't forget to throw in a few *red herrings*. Maybe you want to shift suspicion to a minor character, such as a friend who suddenly has a lot of money to spend on video games. Later it is discovered that the friend got the money from working at a part-time job that he or she kept secret. Also, remember that suspense is a key ingredient in a mystery story. So, use the element of surprise often. Make the readers expect one thing, and give them something else. And, allow your main character and the minor characters to be scared. This builds tension and involves the audience directly in the suspense.

Finally, as you write the story, be sure to include descriptive language that creates a mood—creaking floors; footsteps in the hall; dark, cold stairwells; scratches in the walls at night; blood-curdling screams; and so on. And, a good storm, with lightning and thunder, always adds a goosebump or two.

### Working with Words

One of the tools a good writer uses is descriptive language; that is language that engages the senses so that the reader can actually be in the scene with the characters in the story. Use of descriptive language is also a technique that writers use to set the mood and create suspense, key elements of any good mystery. Have you ever thought about how the choice of an adjective or even a noun can elicit a specific mood or suggest a type of certain kind of event?

For example, if I created a list of words taken from a newspaper story and asked you to guess what the story was about, do you think you could? Let's give it a try.

Here are the word clues taken from a newspaper story:

*forgery*    *accounts*    *victims*    *arrested*    *computers*

If you guessed that the story was about a theft ring whose members were *arrested* for stealing *computers*, credit cards, and stolen-check *forgery*, draining hundreds of *victims'* bank *accounts*, you would be correct. Of course, it was easy to surmise that this had to be a story dealing with the crime of forgery from the word clues. Now, try to guess again using these words:

*reckless surprise faster weekend crashes*

You might think these word clues are taken from a story about a car accident, which is a good guess, but not correct. The story is actually from the sports section; it is about a World Cup Slalom race in which a skier, known for his *reckless* style that often leads to *crashes*, took a *surprise* second place in the *weekend* races.

## Reconstructing the Context

Reconstructing a story from key words can help students recognize that some words have strong associations with certain contexts. That is because we often see them in that context more than any other. For example, the word *forgery* is usually associated with a crime, so the context of the first story was easier to reconstruct. However, *reckless*, which means a lack of thought about the danger that may be involved, while often used in the context of driving and automobile accidents, is used in the story about the World Cup Slalom to refer to the skier's style. Many students have trouble recognizing words out of their familiar surroundings. To help students build their understanding of word use across different contexts, try an activity similar to the previous examples. You will first need to collect articles from different sections of the newspaper. Cut the stories out and paste them onto poster board. Choose about six to eight words, depending on the length of the story, and create a list of word clues for each story. Highlight these words in the newspaper story. Number each story and its word list with the same number for easy identification. Have students choose a list of word clues and reconstruct a story using those words. After they have completed their reconstructed story, give them the newspaper story for comparison. Many students are surprised that the stories are so different. This comparison provides students with examples of how words can be used to construct various meanings in different contexts.

## Connecting across the Curriculum

A good mystery is really like a jigsaw puzzle. The puzzle pieces, like clues, have to be put together in such a way that all the parts fit. Only when all the pieces are assembled in their proper places can we see the complete picture. If a puzzle piece is missing, the picture is incomplete. One can only guess what the puzzle piece might look like in view of the whole image being represented. History has left us with many such puzzles. The missing pieces, those bits of information that have been left out of the historical record for various reasons, have been the source of countless hypotheses that people have proposed as solutions to unexplained phenomena.

### Searching for Clues from the Past

The unexplained mysteries taken from the disciplines of history and science have been the subject of many books, documentary television programs, and films. The construction of the ancient pyramids, the disappearance of the Inca and Anasazi civilizations, the origin and purpose of Stonehenge, all have been studied, and possible answers have been proposed. You can extend your genre study of mystery into the content areas of history and science through inquiry into some of these unexplained mysteries.

To prepare students for their own research, I begin with an example that is based on historical or scientific fact that has been researched by experts in the field. For example, the case of the mass deaths that occurred in the Jamestown colony continues to be the subject of inquiry for historians and others interested in this puzzling phenomenon. From the beginning, the Jamestown colony seemed cursed. After setting sail from London, the colonists were stranded for weeks off the British coast, which resulted in the depletion of precious food and water. During the voyage, many died. When they finally reached the shores of Virginia, they decided to set up their colony in an area that was then a peninsula, now an island that is very swampy. Almost immediately they were plagued with disease, internal strife, and attacks from the Algonquin. The winter of 1610 proved devastating for the colonists. Of the 500, only 60 survived. There has been much speculation about why so many perished. The most popular theory attributes their demise to drought and lack of food, causing them to starve to death. A recent theory links the deaths to arsenic poisoning perpetrated by operatives of the Spanish government in order to get rid of the English colony. Another theory is that the deaths were the result of plague brought on by an infestation of black rats, which theorists think were aboard the ship, since this species was only found in Europe at that time. Whatever the cause, the mystery is still unsolved.

After providing an example that has several theories explaining the phenomena, provide a list of other mysteries that students can choose from to conduct their own inquiries. Three of the most popular are:

- **The Statues of Easter Island**

  Located on an isolated island in the South Pacific off the western South American coast some 3700 kilometers, these statues have prompted questions about the people who made them. What is the significance of their unique form? How did they come to rest at the edge of the island, far away from where they were carved?

- **The Nazca Lines of Peru**

  Located in the hot desert of southwest Peru, huge geometric patterns and spirals, as well as animal figures, are carved into the surface of the desert. These lines have mystified scientists since their discovery in the 1920s. From the ground, they are an undefined mass of lines, but from the air, the figures come to life. Who made them and for what purpose?

## • Stonehenge

High above the Salisbury Plain in Wiltshire, England, rests the massive monument called Stonehenge. The *stones* of the main monument form layers of circles that gradually enclose the site. The *henge*, a banked ditch, surrounds the circle and a pathway leads from the northeast side of the monument to the River Avon. What is this monument? Historians, astronomers, and archaeologists continue to debate the question.

There are many more unexplained phenomena that can provide interesting topics for student inquiries, ranging from black holes in space to UFO sightings in Roswell, New Mexico.

### What's in a Name: Finding Connections with Your Past

In the novel, Consuelo wants to be called by her real name rather than an Americanized version, Connie, that her Anglo grandmother Grace uses. When Grace introduces her granddaughter as Connie to Isabella, Consuelo adamantly proclaims her name as Maria Consuelo Harburton, shouting, "And please call me Consuelo!" Names are important to everyone; they are part of defining who you are. For the heroine in *Call Me Consuelo*, calling her a name other than her own, real name strikes at the core of her history, where she has come from and who she is. In many societies, names hold spiritual and prophetic significance. What a child is named, therefore, will affect her or his future endeavors. For example, the people of Ghana believe that a name is a religious mark of identification and carries with it a sign of honor and respect. A good name is therefore highly treasured in Ghanaian society. A name is given to a child at a naming ceremony. Different cultures conduct these ceremonies in various ways.

To extend the idea of the importance of names, students can conduct inquiries into their own names—who they were named after, the origin of the name, any prophecy associated with the name, and so forth. Many surnames have family crests, symbols representing origins and meanings behind a family's name. Some of these crests are symbolic of a trade or craft that the family was known for. For example, my grandfather's family crest has two hammers that represent the craft of metallurgy. Students can develop a crest for first names to represent the meanings behind their given first names.

Students can also extend the concept of the importance of names by researching the different kinds of naming ceremonies that are still practiced in societies around the world. Many students may have been a part of such formal rituals themselves. There are also many family traditions that accompany the naming of a new baby. Ask students to write about the traditions and rituals for naming that are practiced in their own families. They may want to include any artifacts, such as an announcement or program of the ceremony, as part of the final project.

## Summary

*Call Me Consuelo* provides an example of a mystery plot that can engage readers on different levels. On one level, as a type of realistic fiction, mystery is highly popular with young adult readers, offering even the most reluctant readers opportunities to engage in a good, suspenseful story. A mystery plot, with its various devices that promote prediction and synthesis and interpretation of clues, helps readers develop these important strategies that can transfer to other types of fiction as well as nonfiction texts. On another level, this novel is accessible to readers who may require a fairly easy reading level. Yet, the plot and subject matter are at a level suitable for older readers, which is often difficult to find in chapter books. As such, this novel is a good transitional text for Limited English Proficient (LEP) and ESOL readers. At a final level, and perhaps most important, *Call Me Consuelo* provides readers with a subplot that can open up discussions about the relationship between language, culture, and identity, and how these affect many people with life experiences that are similar to those of the heroine in the story. Thus, the intertwining of the mystery plot and the embedded subplot that presents a diverse perspective on real issues make the novel a good choice to include in a genre study of realistic fiction.

# Chapter 4

## *Jumping Off to Freedom:*
## Fiction from Today's Headlines

### Story Summary

The story of *Jumping Off to Freedom* is one of hope and a struggle for freedom from Castro's oppressive dictatorship in Cuba. The plot is divided into two basic parts. The first part describes the preparation for "jumping off," a slang term for escaping from Cuba by rafting to southern Florida. In the second part, the dangerous journey at sea aboard the makeshift raft unfolds. In the opening chapter, we meet David Leal and his family as they are enmeshed in the events of David's arrest and detention in jail. It all begins when David's bicycle is found at the scene of a crime—the slaughtering of a cow, which is government property in Cuba. David's friend Pepe, who had asked to borrow David's bicycle, is caught red-handed at the scene of the crime. There are rumors that Pepe's accomplice, someone named Tomás Pico, ran away to save his own skin, leaving Pepe alone to face imprisonment of at least seven or eight years. After many hours of interrogation, David is finally released and is allowed to return home.

One night, David is awakened from sleep by what he thinks are burglars. It is common for thieves to steal things to sell on the black market. Armed with a baseball bat and ready to confront the thieves, David finds his father, Miguel, packing boards into their old garage. David soon discovers Miguel's plan to build a raft to escape from Cuba. Rosa, David's mother, is against the plan and refuses to go, fearing that they will die at sea. But Miguel convinces David that "jumping off" is the only hope that their family has to live in freedom. When they reach the safety of Florida, they will be able to make an official request for Rosa and David's little sister, Diana, to join them in the United States. David agrees that this plan will work and joins in the preparation for the journey.

The day of departure arrives. Luis, who has gotten a "passport," secures a place on the raft through his contribution of building supplies. Luis arrives at the beach in a truck with Toro, a mean-spirited man who has plans to jump aboard at the last minute. As they are towing the raft to the water, the truck gets stuck on a rock. Miguel and David know this will endanger their escape. With the truck in plain view on the beach, State Security will know a raft has been launched and will soon alert the Border Guard to track them down in their fast boat. As the men rush to launch the raft so they can put as much distance between them and the Guard, Toro jumps aboard. He tells them that the truck was assigned to him, and he has no choice. And neither do Miguel and David, because Toro blackmails them into letting him stay. After all, if he is left behind, he will have to give the Border Guard *something* to save his skin when he is caught. And, there is no doubt that the something will be the names of the men on the raft. With that, Miguel, David, Luis, and Toro set off for southern Florida, although they are unprepared for the dangers ahead.

From the first night, the men live in constant fear of discovery by the Border Guard, who have been known to sink rafts, leaving the rafters to die in the ocean. This is not the only danger that the crew faces, however. David is the first to suffer seasickness. Luis and Miguel soon become ill, too. They are unable to eat, and their vomiting may dehydrate them. Eating and drinking are essential for survival, and the men need to maintain their strength to navigate and sail the raft. The seriousness of the crew's seasickness becomes more evident as the journey continues. On the second day out, they spot a gunboat on the horizon and are convinced that State Security has found the truck and has sent the Border Guard to look for them. But, the gunboat is not the only danger

on the horizon. A storm is also brewing, and within minutes the little raft is being tossed about by an increasingly rolling sea. Thunder and lightning flash all around, and the crew is hammered with
sheets of rain and wind. Afraid they will be washed overboard they
have to hold onto the raft as it slides down the ocean swells. As
night falls, the storm begins to subside and everyone has survived,
but much of the food, including some of the fresh water, has been
lost. To make matters worse, sharks are sighted following the raft.

With limited supplies, the men become physically weaker, and
their tempers begin to flare, pitting Toro against the rest of the
crew, particularly David. Luis, in his weakened state, is becoming
more and more incoherent and can no longer take care of himself. Eventually, David's father, Miguel, slips into unconsciousness.
After a cargo ship passes the little raft without helping them, even
Toro falls victim to total despair. It is then that David realizes that
if the men are to survive, he will have to assume the responsibility for getting the raft and its crew to the safety of Florida shores.
In a series of events in which Toro exhibits bravery by saving the
lives of both David and Luis, David begins to see another side of
the man, a courageous and unselfish side, and he starts to change
his mind about Toro, who he has discovered is really Tomás Pico.
The story ends as David calls his mother with the news that they
have landed in the Florida Keys.

### Building Background Before You Read

### Cuba Is More Than an Island

When we think of Cuba, we often associate it with the large
island that is situated just to the south of Florida. The Republic of
Cuba actually consists of an archipelago, a group or chain of
many islands, located within a larger group of islands called the
Greater Antilles. You may remember from Chapter 2 that Puerto
Rico is also part of this island group, along with Jamaica and the
island of Hispaniola, shared by Haiti and the Dominican Republic. To the northeast of the Greater Antilles are the Bahamas. The

archipelago of Cuba consists of the large island that constitutes the mainland and more than a thousand smaller islands, islets, keys, and capes that can be divided into four main groups. These groups are the Archipelago of Santa Isabel, the Archipelago of Sabana-Camagüey, the Archipelago of Jardines de la Reina, and the Archipelago of Los Canarreos. The combined archipelago of Cuba is situated just south of the Tropic of Cancer in the Atlantic Ocean, at the entrance to the Caribbean and the Gulf of Mexico. In *Jumping Off to Freedom,* we read about the close proximity of some of these island groups and where they rest in relation to Cuban waters. For example, on page 87 of the text, Cay Sal is referred to as a possible resting spot for the rafters. However, because the small island has no fresh water and the Border Guard makes raids on many of the small neighboring Bahamian islands even though they are outside of Cuban jurisdiction, the stop can only be a short one. A good way to provide students with a visual orientation to the waters around the Cuban Archipelago, the Florida Keys, and the neighboring island groups is through the use of a nautical chart or map. As students read about the raft journey, they can also plot a possible course that might have taken the characters in the novel to their final point of entry into the United States, which was one of the Florida Keys (p. 197).

Another physical feature important to the story is the Gulf Stream. Referred to as a "wide flowing river" (p. 87), it acts as a kind of conveyer belt and navigational aid that naturally pushes the raft in the direction of Florida. The Gulf Stream is actually a western boundary current, which means that it flows along the west side of the major ocean basin of the North Atlantic. Western boundary currents are a result of the interaction of ocean basin topography with the direction of the prevailing winds and the motion of the ocean's water, which is influenced by the rotation of the Earth. Western boundary currents are primarily known for their strength, due to the high velocity of flow and the amount of water being carried through a narrow basin. These currents also play a major role in the overall dynamics of the ocean basins, as well as determining regional climate. The warm waters transported by the Gulf Stream have a moderating effect on the climate of the United Kingdom and neighboring countries of continental Europe.

## Historical Overview

Like Puerto Rico and the neighboring islands in the Atlantic Ocean and Caribbean Sea, Cuba shares a history of conquest and colonization by the Spanish. The indigenous people who inhabited the Cuban archipelago at the time of Columbus's arrival were Taínos, similar to the Taíno inhabitants of Puerto Rico. As the Taíno population of the islands of Cuba diminished, African slaves were brought to the island to supply the labor force for work in the gold and copper mines as well as the sugar and tobacco fields. By the latter part of the eighteenth century, Cuban society was organized along racial and class lines: whites, either *peninsulares* or creoles born in Cuba, mulattos (racially mixed), free blacks, and black slaves. In present-day Cuba, the population reflects this multiracial history and includes other ethnic groups, such as Chinese, Haitians, and descendants of southern and eastern European immigrants.

Although Cuba remained under Spanish rule until 1898, Cuba and the United States began developing an economic and political relationship early on in the U.S. history. During the late 1700s and early 1800s, trade began to flourish as demands for sugar, tobacco, and coffee increased in both the United States and Europe. Conversely, because most of Cuba's farmland had been cultivated for these export crops, Cuba had to rely on the importation of basic food products and other supplies from the United States. As trade increased, divisions among Cuban society became more distinct. Fearing a revolution like the one in Haiti, which resulted in a black republic, many of the free Cubans, who were also wealthy landowners, became fearful of a similar experience and sought reforms from the Spanish colonial government. Others began to think of annexation by the United States. Still others wanted independent status. By 1824, Spain's only holdings in the Americas were Cuba, Puerto Rico, and the Virgin Islands. With the proclamation of the

Monroe Doctrine in December 1823, came the declaration of U.S. support of the governments in places throughout the New World, which, in effect, upheld the rights of the newly independent republics against foreign intervention and also maintained the rights of Spanish rule over Cuba. However, Cuban nationalists continued to seek independence, and various rebellions took place, the most notable being the Ten Years War (1868–1878). Although the Spanish armies defeated the guerilla revolutionary forces, the tone was set for the masses of Cuba to cry out for democracy and the abolition of slavery. In 1880, the Cortes—the Spanish Parliament—approved an abolition law; however, they attached a *patronato* period. During this eight-year period, liberated slaves would have to serve their former masters as indentured servants. In 1886, slavery was totally abolished. Meanwhile, private investors from the United States were becoming a part of many sectors of the Cuban economy, such as the tobacco and sugar plantations, the iron and oil fields, and even public utilities.

In 1895, Cuban nationalists, led by Jose Martí, declared a war of independence from Spanish rule. Martí, a lawyer as well as a journalist and poet, in addition to writing literary works that inspired a spirit of revolution, organized political support in both Cuba and the United States. This support was geared toward the overthrow of Spanish rule. Even when Martí was killed in the conflict at Dos Ríos, his death did not deter the movement toward independence. The battles continued on both sides. Cuban revolutionaries and Spanish colonialists were responsible for widespread human casualties and deaths as well as destruction of property. Finally, when riots broke out in Havana, representatives of the United States in Cuba called for protection of U.S. property and economic interests, and the United States deployed the battleship U.S.S. Maine to Havana Harbor. On February 15, 1898, the U.S.S. Maine mysteriously exploded and sank, and all of the crew was lost. The incident provoked the United States into a declaration of war against Spain on April 25, 1898. The Cuban revolutionaries, who had originally wanted only political recognition and economic aid from the United States, now accepted military intervention in hopes this would aid their independence. However, the United States entered the war without recognizing the Republic of Cuba.

With the United States' victory over Spain came the occupation of Cuba. Although the U.S. government allowed Cuba to elect local officials, draft a constitution, set in place a bicameral legislature, and elect a president, the passage of the Platt Amendment by the U.S. Congress resulted in essentially tying Cuba to U. S. political and economic interests and preventing Cuba from becoming a self-determining country. It was not until 1933, when sergeant Fulgencio Batista y Zaldívar organized a revolt, that the course of Cuban history changed. Batista went on to become president of Cuba and remained in power for the next twenty-five years either as president or the power behind the scenes while others held the presidency. Batista returned to the presidency after a 1952 coup and ruled as a dictator until he was overthrown by the forces of the Cuban Revolution of 1959, led by Fidel Castro.

Initially, the United States recognized the new Cuban government. However, soon the new government began to enact laws and policies that affected U. S. interests in Cuba. One such law was the Agrarian Reform Law, which expropriated farmlands that were over 1000 acres and would not permit foreign land ownership. Subsequent events, such as the confiscation of U.S.-owned oil refineries and other properties by the Cuban government, resulted in the United States imposing an economic embargo on Cuba. U.S. President Dwight D. Eisenhower's breaking off diplomatic relations with Cuba in January 1961, was the first in a series of political events that have set United States-Cuba policies for decades. The next important event occurred on April 17, 1961, when a brigade of Cuban exiles, approved by President John Kennedy, trained by the Central Intelligence Agency (C.I.A.) and armed with U.S. weapons, invaded Cuba at the Bay of Pigs in an attempt to overthrow the government. The attempt failed, but the act escalated the tensions between the countries, and in October, 1962, U.S. aerial reconnaissance photographs revealed the installation of offensive nuclear missiles by Russian technicians. Many of us remember those tense thirteen days in October that have been labeled the "Cuban Missile Crisis" in history textbooks.

The United States and Cuba have generally maintained an adversarial relationship marked by economic sanctions by the United States against Cuba and prohibitions on travel by United States citizens to Cuba. Immigration policies have, at times, allowed Cubans entry into the United States and at other times, particularly recently, closed the doors to refugees. With the dissolution of the Soviet Union came the termination of Soviet economic subsidies and, in turn, the economic well-being of all of Cuba's citizens. The resulting rationing of food and inadequacies of social and public services are addressed in the story of *Jumping Off to Freedom*. Another real-life issue that plays an important part in the book is the treatment of human rights in Cuba. The descriptions of David's arrest, imprisonment, and interrogation give the reader a glimpse into the conditions that many Cuban citizens face when they are charged with a crime for which they are assumed guilty. This is directly opposite to the rights of U.S. citizens that guarantee the accused party's innocence until proven guilty by a trial before a jury of one's peers. Over the past decades, the rule over Cuban citizens has been a cycle of repression that has at times been severe and at other times relaxed, depending on the economic trade relations with other countries, among other factors. The repression of political dissidents, those who publicly criticize the government, has not only restricted freedoms of speech, press, and public assembly, but it has also resulted in these political prisoners' unfair trials and subjection to inhuman prison conditions.

Because of the repressive political and economic conditions that have had adverse effects on the citizens of Cuba, many people, like the characters in the book *Jumping Off to Freedom*, have attempted to escape by raft or boat to the United States. One organization, Brothers to the Rescue, which was founded in 1991, provides assistance to those people who are struggling to gain freedom. The organization is a small nonprofit corporation that flies humanitarian missions searching for rafters in the Florida Straits. The organization is made up of volunteers from various countries, including Argentina, Peru, France, Jamaica, the United States, and Puerto Rico. Besides aerial search missions, Brothers to the Rescue has conducted flights to drop food, water, and supplies of medicine and clothing to deserted Bahamian islands (like the one mentioned in the story). It has also made deliveries of supplies to a Cuban refugee detention camp in Nassau, Bahamas.

A good way to stimulate interest in the historical and political backdrop for the book is to have students create a timeline of important events involving the United States and Cuba. By listing the events that have influenced present-day relations between the countries, students can begin to link the direct consequences on the economic and political conditions affecting the citizens of Cuba that are highlighted in the text. The chronological summary can also provide topics for research that can serve to extend students' learning after they read *Jumping Off to Freedom.*

## Reading and Responding to the Story

In *Jumping Off to Freedom,* the main characters' daily lives are filled with oppressive and adverse conditions with which most of us living in the United States have no knowledge or experience. As law-abiding citizens of the United States, we enjoy the freedom to travel from city to city, state to state, without any travel papers or fear of arrest and interrogation by government authorities, without any apparent cause. We enjoy the freedom of speech, and do not have to talk to our relatives and friends in a secret code for fear of reprisal by a government that may be listening to our phone conversations. We are also granted the right of being innocent of a crime until proven guilty. The characters in the story, as citizens of Cuba, do not enjoy such rights. For this reason, people like David and Miguel Leal risk their lives to have a chance to live in a free country. The dangers that the real-life Cuban rafters face on the open sea are similar to those presented in the book. Besides the constant threat of being discovered by the Cuban Border Guard, the rafters must survive the perilous conditions of an unforgiving sea and the creatures that live in it. Barely equipped for the voyage and unprepared for the conditions Mother Nature can whip up, they set out on crudely assembled, open rafts that can break apart in rough seas. The waters between Cuba and Florida where the Gulf Stream runs at a fast rate can often be subject to squalls that produce turbulent seas with steep swells and high winds and waves. My husband and I have done some bluewater cruising in a sturdy, 40-foot sailboat, and the thought of riding out a storm on an open, poorly constructed raft, is something I am sure I would not have the mettle to face. In the two settings in which the action takes place, in Cuba and on the raft, the characters are faced with difficult obstacles, sometimes under perilous conditions. In both settings, they face these with courage and determination. This is a reality that many people living in Cuba today experience as part of their daily lives.

To prepare students to think critically about the conditions described in the story as they relate to their own lives, ask students to complete this prompt before you begin reading.

The most dangerous or difficult thing I ever had to do was . . .

I often have students create a response journal specifically for this book using folded blank letter-sized copy paper either stapled together on the seam or hole-punched in two places along the spine, tied with twine to simulate the rope that the men had on the raft. For the cover, I copy a section of a nautical chart that shows the waters between Cuba and the Florida Keys. Some libraries have nautical charts, or you may know someone who has charts of that particular area. If you cannot find a chart, a copy of a map that shows the Caribbean Sea and Cuba and Florida will work. Make sure the chart or map is larger than the journal paper so the ends can be folded down onto the outer piece of journal paper and glued to make a cover. This themed journal not only creates interest for students, it also provides an authentic physical orientation for the settings.

## Describing the Sociopolitical and Economic Conditions

In the first part of the story (pages 9 through 75), set in Cuba, the author describes the sociopolitical and economic conditions that affect the characters' everyday lives, which are part of living in a socialist system of government. As students read the first part of the story, ask them to record their observations of the conditions described in the text. The observations can first be recorded chronologically, listing the condition and the page number.

For example:

| Page # | Condition |
|--------|-----------|
| 12 | *Gasoline and auto parts are minimal since Russian supply has been cut off; public vehicles in bad condition; transportation is mostly on Chinese bicycles, which are expensive, which means limited ownership.* |
| 13 | *Beating prisoners during interrogation session by police officials is common.* |

After you have read and responded to the first part of the story, a good review of the events that lead up to the second part is to create categories for the different conditions students have recorded in their journals. Categorizing data such as the "conditions" students recorded in their journals is an organizational strategy similar to a preliminary stage of analysis that many qualitative researchers apply to the data they have collected. This is often referred to as *coding*. For example, the "condition" on page 12 deals with issues of transportation. Since others related to transportation appear on page 17 (cattle trucks were used as buses and thirty-year-old cars were used as taxis for tourists), and additional references can be found on pages 25, 40, 55, and 66, *transportation* would be a good category heading. Other categories for the "conditions" described in the text that have emerged from my own class discussions about this book are: *crimes and punish-*

*ments* (crimes, arrest procedures, jail sentences, prison conditions), *black market* (goods sold), and *public services* (electricity and
telephone service, food rationing).

## Making Critical Comparisons

To extend this organizational/analytical activity into a critical
comparison that relates the textual reading to the student's life
experience, students can create a list of the conditions in the United States for comparison with conditions in Cuba. For example,
using the category *transportation*, a list might include *commuter
trains, subway trains, buses, individually owned cars,* and *airplanes.*

## Keeping a Ship's Log

The second part of the story (from page 75 to the end) is primarily set aboard the raft. Many of the terms used have a nautical
meaning—*tiller, radar, boom, current, launch,* to name a few. Likewise, the description of the journey is filled with events that happen often while sailing on the ocean in a boat. To be sure, the
danger to the characters in the story and the real-life rafters is
greatly compounded by the lack of a seaworthy vessel, a limited
food and water supply, the absence of any kind of navigation
equipment or charts, and the constant threat posed by the Border
Guard. Still, all sailors must navigate to arrive at their desired destination. David used the North Star as his navigation aid. Navigation usually involves plotting a course on an ocean chart and
maintaining that course toward the final destination. Today, many
sailors have a Global Positioning System (GPS) that tells exact longitude and latitude positions. This has replaced the traditional
way of determining a vessel's position with a *sextant.* Steering the
course is done with *tiller.* If you remember, the raft in the story has
a tiller, and the crew takes turns in steering the course. The tiller
is attached to a *rudder,* which is an underwater device that can
point the boat in different directions. A tiller does the same thing
as a ship's wheel, which is much like a steering wheel in a car. The
only difference is that with a tiller, if you turn the tiller to the right

or *starboard,* your rudder will turn left, the exact opposite, and your boat will turn to the left or *port.* Sailors also adjust the sails to get the most out of the wind's power. The men on the raft had to adjust their sail—putting it up to catch a breeze and taking it down in the storm. Riding out stormy weather and rough seas as well sighting sharks and other marine life are also common occurrences. And, yes, many sailors suffer from seasickness.

Traditionally, events occurring on ocean voyages are documented in a *ship's log,* which is similar to a journal. Typical entries would include a recording of the day/date and time, latitude and longitude position, the course heading or compass reading, wind speed, boat speed, weather conditions, and sightings, such as other boats or marine life. As students read the second part of the story, ask them to keep a ship's log, summarizing each day's (both day and evening) events at sea. Entries can be written from the point of view of one of the characters in the text, or students may choose to write from the point of view of an observer. Although exact times are not provided in the text, the events are described as happening either in the daytime or at night. Students can create an approximate time of day or night the event occurred for their log entries. I have taught students to use marine or military time designations in local time for their entries, like 0800, 1500, 2100, and so on. This is really very simple. If you start with 12 midnight, the military equivalent is 2400. As you move around the clock then, 1 a.m. is 0100, 2 a.m. is 0200, and so on. Ten o'clock a.m. is 1000—there is no zero prefix, and it is the same for eleven, 1100, and twelve noon, 1200. Then, for every hour after 1200, you add 100. So, 1 o'clock p.m. becomes 1300, 2 p.m. is 1400, and so on till you reach midnight, and you start all over again. Minutes are recorded in 60-minute increments—like civilian time. So, for example, if you wanted to record the time of 1:30 a.m., then the military equivalent would be 0130. For log entries, daylight hours would be roughly between 0500 and 1800 hours, and evening would be somewhere between 1900 and 0400 hours. Using the events of the first night out, here is an example of a log entry.

| Time | Weather/Sea Conditions | Event/Sighting |
|------|------------------------|----------------|
| 1900 | No moon, stars out, clear night | City lights, shrimp boat |
|      | | Border Guard checks out shrimper |
|      | Light breeze, calm seas | Miguel at tiller first with Toro and David oaring and Luis on watch |
| 2300 | | David takes tiller with Miguel and Luis at oars and Toro on watch |

**Figure 4-1.** Ship's Log Entry

I usually model the first log entry to help students understand the process as well as provide strategies that help readers infer and construct meaning from the information given in the text. For example, as a whole group, begin the activity by reading aloud the first night's events as presented on pages 75–82. Then, on a blank overhead with the categories listed above, ask students to provide a probable time the events may have occurred. For example, the text provides the information that they had launched the raft at dark so the Border Guard would not see them. Therefore, it was probably in the early evening that the city lights were turned on. From the text we can also infer that it was a clear night because there were stars out. And, the "invisible waves" that "lapped" on the sides of the raft (p. 78) indicate that the seas were fairly calm, probably with a gentle breeze blowing. The new time entry, 2300, reflects an inference that time would have lapsed between the first *watch*—steering, rowing, and lookout duties—and the second watch.

After students have completed reading and recording entries in their logs, a good summarizing activity is to create a timeline of the raft journey. This activity provides students with a review of the sequence of events and a self-assessment rubric to check their entries for completeness and accuracy, as well as their inferencing skills.

## To Go or Not to Go

One of the issues discussed in the story centers on the decision

to stay in Cuba and live under difficult and often oppressive conditions or risk the dangers of "jumping off" to a better life in the
United States. When David first discovers his father's plans for
building a raft and leaving Cuba, he assumes that his whole family
will be making the journey. However, Miguel tells David that Rosa
refuses to go, and Diana, David's little sister, is staying with her.
The two parents present their arguments (beginning on page 34)
in an effort to influence David's decision—Miguel wants David to
go with him and Rosa wants him to stay with her. Should David go
or should he stay? After reading the story, students should be
familiar with the conditions outlined in the book and possible
consequences involved in each choice. To extend the reading, students can prepare and conduct an informal debate. I usually
divide students into debate teams of four. If you are reading the
texts using a literature circle approach, this grouping also works
well. Each team prepares arguments representing the two different perspectives. Knowing both sides of the argument is essential
to a good debate, because it helps the debater anticipate the
counter-argument that the opposing team may present. An important strategy for debating is presentation of known, or "factual"
information, rather than opinion, and being able to use this information in counter arguments to the opposing team. For example,
when Miguel introduces his negative experience with the *agrarian
service* (p. 34), Rosa counters with her more positive one that there
is enough to eat. Miguel then presents the counter argument that
times have changed, and they are grinding up banana peels to
stretch their limited rations (p. 35). Students may want to gather
additional supporting evidence from other sources about such
topics as the agrarian service, food and public utilities rationing,
real-life rafters' experiences, and so on. Online newspapers, ency-
clopedias, and other websites can provide this information.

## Gathering Supplies

In preparation for "jumping off," Miguel and David set about
doing many tasks, including building the raft, assembling sup-

plies, and recording the times the Border Guard go out on patrol. This preparation is essential to the success of the journey. Throughout the first part of the story, parts of the planning process are presented. For example, on page 36, we learn that Miguel has been studying the currents and tides and will keep track of the weather conditions. In Chapter 3, David keeps track of the Border Guard's schedule. Beginning on page 61, the process is complete, and everything is in place for their departure. The raft is described, and a list of supplies is presented in detail. One way to move the written words into the spatial realm of students' experience is to assemble the different supplies that are described on pages 61–62. To begin the process, as a whole class, construct a graphic organizer listing the supplies in the text. You may want to include the names of the students responsible for bringing in the different supplies. Using this checklist, assemble the supplies. These will also serve as *stage props* for the *dramatic tableau* activity described below. The actual gathering of these supplies can bring a dimension of material reality to the book that provides a sobering example of just one of the dangers to survival facing the characters and the real-life rafters: the small amounts of food and water that must last six and sometimes seven days.

## Creating a Dramatic Tableau

Using drama as a way to respond to a book or as a performance assessment is often appealing to teachers as well as students. Incorporating the dramatic arts in the teaching of literature allows students to express themselves creatively and provides an alternative to the usual written assignment. Through drama, readers can move the story from a two-dimensional text to a three-dimensional representation that can extend comprehension through additional support of visual, aural, and spatial modes of learning. This is nothing new to teachers. However, many teachers and students in my children's literature classes have commented that asking students to "act out" a scene from a book or "create a skit" in response to the book often results in confusion and frustration for the students. In addition, the final outcome usually does not adequately portray student learning. This may be due to students' limited experience with actually creating and performing dramatic scenes, which directly affects their ability to use the medium as a way to respond to literature. Just because we go to movies or watch videos at home does not mean that this spectator experience provides us with the knowledge to create and perform a dramatic scene.

One strategy that involves students in creative interpretation without having to create an original script is staging a dramatic *tableau.* A *tableau* is a still image that is created by people assuming a still pose to depict an event or convey an idea or human emotion. I have seen dramatic tableaus representing famous paintings like Da Vinci's *Last Supper* and Grant Wood's *American Gothic.* Dramatic tableaus can also be used to portray literary texts that are read to the audience by a narrator. The first step is to find a passage in the book or story that can lend itself to a still-life presentation. The next step is to stage the scene by designating an area for your tableau and assembling a few key objects that are specifically mentioned in the passage. Finally, actors create a freeze-frame pose that depicts the action described in the text. For example, in *Jumping Off to Freedom,* there are many scenes described in the second part of the story that take place on the raft, which may easily be portrayed through tableaus. The basic *set* for the tableau is an area that represents the raft and some *props* to add a sense of place. Props are those objects that are specifically indicated in the script and also include many additional items that one would normally find in the place where the scene is set. In tableaus, you do not need to have elaborate sets with scenery backdrops like those you find in theatre productions. A few props that are key to the action and careful posing of the actors are all that are needed to give the audience a snapshot of the action of the passage being read by a narrator. For example, using the passage beginning with the fourth paragraph on pages 78 through 79 as the text for the tableau, the props needed would be a pair of oars (these can be real oars or made from cardboard) and a pair of binoculars. The main action of the passage takes place in the paragraph, which begins with, "David clenched his teeth and threatened," on page 79. The actors portraying David and Luis are central, and the action is David grasping Luis's hair and grabbing the cord of the binoculars to take them away from Luis who, in a panic, is endangering the crew on the raft. The actors should practice posing in their positions and try to maintain them while the narrator reads the passage of text being portrayed. A series of different scenes depicted through tableau can be presented as a set. To change sets, dim the lights so that the actors can assume a new pose. Then bring the house lights up on the new scene.

## Working with Words

As you have already discovered, *Jumping Off to Freedom* can be divided into two parts—the preparation and the journey. Each part of the plot takes place in two major settings—in Cuba, and aboard the raft on the ocean, respectively. The events that occur within each part of the story are often described and presented in terms that are specific to that particular setting. For example, in the first part of the story, which takes place in Cuba, there are many terms describing the social and political conditions of Castro's government. Terms such as *socialist system* (p. 10), *black market* (p. 16), and *agrarian service* (p. 34), are examples. The same holds true for the second part of the story that takes place on the ocean. Here, many nautical terms and words related to the ocean are used, such as *tiller* (p. 76), *Gulf Stream* (p. 86), *boom* (p. 91), *sealegs* (p. 93), and *sargassum* (193).

## Read All About It!

As part of the *Reading and Responding* activities in the previous section, students kept a reading log in which they recorded the events and important information embedded in each part of the story—the conditions in present-day Communist Cuba in the first part and the daily events at sea in the second half. They also identified words or terms that were associated with these two sections.

Ask students to review these pages in their logs and compile a class list of the terms they found in each part of the story. Since the story of *Jumping Off to Freedom* is based on historical and political events that have been part of various news stories about Cuba over the last few decades, a different way to have students demonstrate their understanding of the meaning of a word or term is to write a headline containing that word or term.

As a prewriting activity, gather various newspapers for examples of headlines. Many major papers have online editions. Writing a good headline requires skill to capture the essence of the story it is introducing. Many headline writers for newspapers begin with one or two key words and then fill in the rest of the needed words, such as adjectives, adverbs, or verbs. Some begin with a complete sentence then shorten it into a form called *telegraphic English,* a term that is derived from the way telegraphs are written. This form may consist of a simple subject-verb, a subject-predicate, or subject-verb-object. In all of these cases, it is important to use a strong action verb, and the active voice is preferable to the passive voice. A good news story always contains the answers to the *five Ws—who, what, where, when, why.* A good headline should include the *who* and the *what.* You might want to make a chart or overhead transparency listing these elements, and review them with the class. Now, take a look at the headlines of the various news articles you have collected. As a whole-class activity or in small groups examine, the headlines using these elements as guidelines. How do they measure up? What would make them better?

After reviewing the headlines from the newspapers, try writing some headlines for the different events in the story, using the entries from the students' reading logs. Write the keywords—the vocabulary term and any necessary words to complete a headline that presents the essence of the event in the story. For example, using the term *black market,* a headline might read:

### Man Arrested in Black Market Crime

The strategy of writing headlines not only provides a different way to think about the meaning of the words, it also provides practice in summarizing a scene with a short statement, which captures its holistic essence. Writing a headline also reinforces comprehension of the text. In order to write an effective and accurate headline, the reader needs to know what happened in the passage being described.

## Connecting across the Curriculum

Perhaps some of you can remember those tense thirteen days in October 1962, when television and radio news programs announced a possible nuclear conflict with Russia over the stationing of missiles in Cuba. It was a serious and sobering moment in history, and many feared that life as we knew it would end with both sides "pushing the button." The "Cuban Missile Crisis" was a result of the tensions that had escalated between the Russia and the United States over Cuba since the time when President Eisenhower had broken off diplomatic relations with Cuba and cut off trade. This act has continued to frame the Cuba-United States political and economic policy for the last 40-plus years.

## Comparing the American Democratic System to the Cuban Socialist System

In the section *Making Critical Comparisons,* students categorized and compared various social and economic conditions with their own experiences of living in the United States. A good way to build on this activity and extend students' thinking in terms of the political arena is to lead students into an inquiry that compares the socialist form of government that is in place in Cuba today with the democratic system of government in the United States. For example, as United States citizens, we know that our founding statesmen developed a Constitution that outlines our rights as citizens as well as defines our governing system. Did you know that Cuba also has a constitution? The current constitution was drafted in 1976 and was heavily amended in 1992 by the National Assembly, which was controlled by the Cuban Communist Party—*Partido Comunista de Cuba* (PCC). The Cuban Constitution provides a framework for the government of Cuba as a socialist workers' republic under a unitary system of government organized along Marxist-Leninist principles. In its ideal form that was presented in the *Communist Manifesto* by Karl Marx and Friedrich Engels, there are no more social classes and no coercive government structures. In the economic structure, everyone has equal access to goods and services because the control of production rests in the hands of the workers who invest their labor without an oppressive ruling class. In other words, everyone shares in the economic wealth, because everyone works and everyone's work is equally valuable. However, this theory did not play out in actual practice in Cuba. When the revolutionary leaders took over in January 1959, they promised the citizens of Cuba a voice in *their* government through elections. However, despite these promises of elections, Cuba has not had a democratically elected government since 1952. Cuba does have elections, but there is only one party, the PCC, and the candidates run unopposed; there is no alternative offered to the ruling Communist Party. This means that in practice the *totalitarian-socialist* regime, which is governed under the single-party rule of the PCC, looks very similar to the Communist bureaucratic regime of the former Soviet Union.

A good place to start your comparison is with the development of parallel KWL charts. Begin with the familiar and list all of the things you know about the government of the United States. For example, most students respond with these facts: the U.S. is a democracy; it has a written constitution; its three branches of government are the executive, legislative, and judicial; every citizen is guaranteed certain inalienable rights, and so forth. This list will provide a starting point for a discussion about what students already know about the Cuban system of government. Generally, many students have limited knowledge about the Cuban government, apart from its definition as Communist-controlled under the leadership of Fidel Castro. Your parallel KWL might look something like this:

| What We KNOW About the U.S. | What We KNOW About Cuba |
|---|---|
| Democracy | Communist ruled |
| President is leader | Fidel Castro is dictator/leader |
| Holds multiparty elections | |
| Constitution | |
| 3 Branches of government | |
| Bill of Rights | |

**Figure 4-2.** Parallel KWL Chart

From this initial brainstorming discussion and comparison, a set of inquiry questions can be developed for the **Want to Know** section of your parallel charts. For example, what are the exact duties and responsibilities of each branch of the U.S. government? Are there comparable branches represented in the Cuban government? What are the specific rights granted to U.S. citizens? Is there a comparable document such as the "Bill of Rights" that lists rights granted to Cuban citizens? The next step is to do the research to find answers to your questions. I have found that forming research teams of two to three students around areas of interests works well. There are many websites available that provide information about the governments of the United States and Cuba. However, be sure to check the sources and references listed for indicators of accurate information.

If your students are literate in Spanish, you can obtain a copy of the Cuban Constitution from various sites on the Web—both the 1976 and 1992 versions—for a direct comparison with the United States Constitution. For access to a copy, type in *Cuban Constitution* for your keyword search. There are also copies of many other countries' constitutions available at various websites, should students want to conduct further comparisons of different forms of government in countries around the world.

## Enacting an Economic Summit

Presently, economic sanctions prohibit trade between the

United States and Cuba. Many of our European allies, such as Spain, Great Britain, France, as well as our border neighbors, Canada and Mexico, have established economic trade policies with Cuba. Even within our country, there are differing viewpoints about these trade agreements, as well as debates concerning the political and economic relations between the United States and Cuba. Two recent Acts of Congress have had some additional effects on U.S. relations with Cuba. The Cuban Democracy Act (1992) created avenues of support for the Cuban people through medical supplies and food donations. It also allowed travel for educational, religious, or journalistic purposes. The Helms Burton Act (1996) essentially transfers the maintenance of economic sanctions from an executive order to a congressional order, thereby requiring any major political shift toward Cuba be enacted through Congress.

A further extension of the comparison between the governments of the United States and Cuba can be developed through a multigenre class research project. This project should be geared toward exploring and comparing the different political and economic policies of countries such as Great Britain, Canada, France, Mexico, and other allies, that are in place with Cuba, with those policies that have been legislated in the United States, such as those identified in the Helms Burton Act.

As a final assessment of their research, ask students to organize and present an enactment of an economic summit meeting that involves the United States and various countries that have trade agreements with the United States and also with Cuba. Students can act as world leaders and present and discuss their respective economic policies toward Cuba and the United States. Students can also play the roles of press reporters, posing questions to the various leaders in a press conference and writing newspaper articles about the summit proceedings. Television newscasts can also be created and recorded on videotape. Both types of media presentations—written articles and television reporting—can also include "man on the street" interviews with citizens from each of these countries providing their views on the different policies.

## Cuban Poster Art: Craft or Propaganda?

In a small country such as Cuba, an efficient and effective way to make political and social messages accessible to a wide range of people is through the medium of posters. Cuban poster art, as in many other countries, began with the appearance of lithographs in the mid-1800s. The development of posters as art grew in tandem with the emergence of a booming film industry in the 1940s. The posters were a means to publicize films to a wide range of moviegoers. Silkscreen printmaking also began to emerge as a fine art form among many Cuban artists. However, it was not until the overthrow of the Batista government by the revolutionary forces of Fidel Castro that a transformation occurred in Cuban poster art. A "golden age" of Cuban posters, followed in the wake of the revolution and was viewed by many as a way that art and artists could assist in creating the social improvements promised by the new socialist government. Most of the posters created and produced in Cuba were products of three agencies. The Organization in Solidarity with the People of Africa, Asia, and Latin America is a non-governmental agency recognized by the United Nations that produces international solidarity posters in Cuba. It has a board of representatives from around the world. The Cuban Film Institute produces posters for Cuban-made films; and the Editora Política, which is the official publishing department of the Cuban Communist Party, is responsible for disseminating a wide range of public information and propaganda through books, brochures, and posters.

Cuban poster art varies widely in content and style. For example, there are posters that promote health services, advocate becoming a teacher, and maintain the building of a socialist community of workers with a call to labor in the sugar industry. Another predominant theme is the call for solidarity against U.S. imperialism and a resistance to colonialism. René Mederos, a prominent

Cuban poster artist, created many posters with such titles as *Viet Nam Will Win; Hiroshima, Anniversary of the Bombing;* and *Nixon Tearing the Heart Out of Indochina.* Mederos also produced posters documenting the history of the Cuban Revolution. Presently there is a website created in conjunction with the University of California Berkeley dedicated to the archival documentation of Cuban poster art. You can access this site, which contains a number of visual images, by typing in the keywords *Cuban poster art.*

Despite the differences in the political tone of some of the messages, here in the United States posters are also used as a means of getting information out to the general public. Some posters announce and publicize films. Think of all the movie posters displayed at your local cinema. There are also posters that are created to send out political and social messages. You may have some in your school that contain messages about the dangers of smoking cigarettes. There are also many national, state, and local poster projects that are designed to involve students of all ages in creating poster art. Many of these are competitions based on important national campaigns or celebrating national events and special days. For example, there are poster competitions for Arbor Day and Earth Day as well as for paying tribute to the work of Dr. Martin Luther King. You may also have local poster projects and competitions that students can enter. Involving students in the creation of posters for a national, state, or local poster project or competition, can provide an authentic link to the concept of poster art as a means for relaying important social messages to a wide range of people, and can generate a real-life connection to the historical purpose of Cuban poster art.

## Summary

The countries of Cuba and the United States have shared a political and economic history for more than 300 years. Over the past forty years, since the takeover of the Cuban government by Fidel Castro, news media headlines and sound bytes have documented an adversarial and hostile relationship between the two countries. Over the course of those forty years, we have read and listened to stories of political dissidence, human rights violations, trade embargoes imposed by the United States, and political policies that act as swinging doors, opening and closing, to Cuban refugees fleeing the island. In *Adrift: The Cuban Raft People,* Alfredo A. Fernández (2000) traces the real-life stories of refugees who were part of a massive wave of migration from Cuba to the United States, which began in 1994 as a direct result of the collapse of the former Soviet Union. With the withdrawal of Soviet economic support came the rationing of basic goods and loss of public services. The ensuing shortages provoked political and social unrest. Riots and protests were common, forcing more governmental control and even less personal freedom for the country's citizens. Faced with such conditions, many Cubans chose to "jump off" in flimsy makeshift rafts across the Florida Straits, bound for freedom in the United States. Although the seas were filled with a steady flow of rafters beginning in 1994, it was not until 1999, with the rescue of Eilían González off the coast of Fort Lauderdale, Florida, that the plight of the Cuban rafters and their families in the United States and in Cuba became a national and international topic in everyday households. In *Jumping Off to Freedom,* we catch a glimpse of the experiences of real people who bravely face separation from family and physical danger for the promise of a better life. However, this is only a point of departure, a "jumping off" place for the ongoing real-life stories of the refugees and countless others remaining in Cuba who continue to be affected by the two governments' political relationship and the resulting policies and economic sanctions. Although the Cuban raft people no longer make the front-page headlines, it is our responsibility as citizens of a country representing an ideal of freedom, for which many risk their very lives, to keep their stories at the forefront of our critical discussions and political debates.

# Chapter 5

## Trino's Choice: The Power of Words

### Story Summary

When we first meet thirteen-year-old Trino Olivares, he is running from Rosca and his gang who have robbed Mr. Epifano at his store. Trino has been playing video games, when suddenly he realizes that the punching and hitting noises he is hearing are not part of the game, but the real sounds of Mr. Epifano getting beaten. Trino gets up just in time to see Rosca hitting Mr. Epifano on the head with a pipe. That is when he ducks into a bookstore, a choice that will change Trino's life. This is an important and pivotal event, because Trino Olivares is living a life he hates. Trino and his three brothers—Felix, Gus and Beto—live in a trailer with his mother and her cousin. Trino's mom works at a motel cleaning rooms, while her *primo*, lazy cousin Garces watches TV and drinks beer all day instead of working.

When Trino is hiding out from Rosca and his gang at Maggie's bookstore, he meets Lisana and her friends, who all go to the same school. They are different from Trino's old friends, Zipper and Rogelio. Lisana and her friends belong to the "school types." They like to read books, even poetry books, which Trino thinks is pretty dumb—that is, until Trino is introduced to Emilce Montoya and his poetry. On his second visit to the bookstore, Trino hears Montoya read his poems. Montoya asks Trino if he knows how to read—really read—which is more than just saying words. It means understanding what the words mean to you. Being able to understand what you are reading matters because if you cannot read and understand, "people tell you what you ought to think, and that you can't do more than scrub toilets the rest of your life" (p. 47). Trino begins to discover that Montoya's words have meaning for him when Montoya gives Trino his personal copy of his book. Despite his strong urge to throw it in the garbage, something inside him will not allow him to do it, and he cannot explain it. Maybe it has something to do with the inscription "Don't let the Man flip the switch and fry you. Read the book!" (p. 49).

Soon after Trino meets Montoya and his new friends, things begin to change at school, especially between Trino and his old friends Zipper and Rogelio. Trino finds himself looking for Lisana and her friends more and more, and enjoys their company and the way they always find things to talk about. It is so different with Zipper and Rogelio. Zipper never says much, and Rogelio always repeats what somebody else has said. Things are also changing at home. Trino's mom is seeing more and more of Nick, a friend from work. Nick buys presents for Trino's little brothers, takes them out for pizza, and even brings home food for Trino's family. Although Trino's mom seems to really like Nick, Trino isn't so sure, and soon Trino begins to resent Nick and his hanging around all the time.

One day, Trino is faced with a very important choice that can affect the rest of his life. Rosca asks him to join him and his gang. The question is, will it be better to be Rosca's friend or his enemy? As far as Trino is concerned, this is not much of a choice—either way, he loses. To make matters worse, Trino comes home one afternoon and finds his Mom home, scrubbing the kitchen floor. She has lost her job at the motel, and now the family has no income to pay the bills. If Trino were only sixteen, he could get a job and help support his family. But, because he is only thirteen, Rosca's proposition begins to look pretty good. He can make some money. Even if it means stealing, at least he will be doing something to help his family.

When Beto becomes ill, it triggers a dramatic chain of events that leads to a climactic ending. It begins when Trino is left in charge of caring for Beto while his mother and Nick go to Tia Sofia's to pick up *caldo*, soup, for his sick brother. While they are gone, Beto's fever gets worse, and Trino cannot find his medicine. By the time his mom and Nick return, Trino has worked himself up into a rage, which results in an argument and a fast exit in search of Rosca.

Catching his breath at the first stall of the car wash, Trino peers around the brick wall to see Zipper and Rogelio along with Rosca and the two boys he saw the day Mr. Epifano was beaten and robbed. Zipper and Rosca are the first to try to force the car-wash vacuum machines open with crowbars. Suddenly, gunshots ring out in the darkness. Rosca is shot in the stomach and Zipper is dead. Rosca tells police that the robbery was Trino's idea and that he supplied the crowbars. Trino tells police that it was Rosca. When Rosca threatens Trino, saying, "I know where you sleep" (p. 106), Trino tells him that if he shows up where he sleeps, he will take care of what is his. Never again will Trino let someone like Rosca do his thinking for him.

Back at school, word is out about Zipper's death. Some kids are saying mean things about his old friend. Mostly, things are going on as if nothing has happened. For Trino, however, nothing is the same. Seeing his friend shot to death has made him feel very lonely and confused. Lisana finds Trino sitting alone at the outside lunch tables at school. Trino tells her about Rosca and Zipper. Hoping that he can trust Lisana to understand, he also tells her that he planned to join Rosca because of his family's need for money, and that he was to blame for Zipper and Rogelio getting mixed up with Rosca in the first place. The story ends with Trino's new choices for his life. He is going to take a job trimming trees with Nick in order to make money for his family. Lisana and Trino make plans to go to a reading by an author at the Book Basket. Trino even begins to feel like school "could be a place where he belonged" (p. 124).

### Building Background Before You Read

One of the themes in *Trino's Choice* is about making choices and living with the consequences of those choices. Another related theme is the power that words have for reflecting on one's experiences and engendering change. Knowing how to read and understand the many meanings that words can convey can open pathways of knowing who you are—your history, your cultural identity—and where you are going. Learning to use words effectively can enable you to communicate with people who are part of your everyday life. Learning how to write your ideas using carefully chosen words gives you the power to tell others who you are and what you believe in. Like Montoya in the story, learning to shape words creatively into powerful messages can help others discover the same power and can open up the potential to enact positive personal and social change. The character of Montoya presents a glimpse into the heritage that is part of the Mexican-American literary tradition. To familiarize students with this tradition, the following brief summary highlights some important contributions that authors and their works have made to contemporary Mexican-American literature and children's literature. The summary is not intended as a complete overview. Rather, it can provide you with points of reference for further reading and research.

The literary tradition of Spanish-speaking peoples in the United States has been influenced by two cultures: that which was introduced through the Spanish conquest and colonization of what is now the United States, and the cultural traditions of the indigenous peoples who populated the regions before the Spanish arrived. Before the first permanent English settlement on the North American continent, literature was written in the Spanish language. Cabeza de Vaca wrote his account of his journey through what became the Gulf Coast states, and de Soto and Coronado published accounts of their expeditions. By 1598, the Oñate colonizing expedition into New Mexico produced not only epic poetry, a genre common to the conquistador tradition, but also produced the first performances of European drama in what is now the United States (Bruce-Novoa, 1990). The Spanish and Hispanicized mestizo and mulatto colonists maintained this Hispanic literary tradition, which began with the writings of the conquistadors, wherever they settled. On the base of this native *mesti-zo* culture in the Southwest, beginning in the late nineteenth century, successive waves of Mexican immigrants also set down roots. This tradition of relocating *al norte* continues to the present.

The 1950s and 1960s brought issues of race and ethnicity to the forefront with the Civil Rights Movement. It was during these decades that the notion of a homogeneous American culture that formed the base of the "melting pot" theory was seriously challenged. While Hispanics have struggled to protect their civil rights since the mid-nineteenth century, a new generation of activists sprang up in the 1960s to adapt some of the same strategies used by the African-American civil rights movement and the anti-Vietnam War activists. The Mexican-American struggle for civil rights in the 1960s and 1970s, sometimes known as the Chicano Movement, spilled over into the literature written by authors within the movement. This writing is characterized by a predominant non-Spanish tone that emphasizes the mixed Indian and Spanish racial background—the *mestizo.*

According to Bruce-Novoa (1990), the Chicano literary movement started with the dramatic works of Luis Valdez's El Teatro Campesino and Rodolfo Corky Gonzales's epic poem *I Am Joaquín.* El Teatro Campesino began as part of César Chávez's United Farm Workers Union. Through its *actos* or skits, the Campesino actors, who were farm workers, presented farm labor problems in a street-theatre format. During this same period, Gonzales, founder of the Crusade for Justice, a community-based activist organization, wrote his famous epic poem, *I Am Joaquín,* first published in 1967. Gonzales, through his recounting of Mexican history, crafts his poem into an instructional tool that presents the struggle by the Mexican people for justice and reclamation of the land that is rightfully theirs.

This approach to writing that drew from Mexican history and archetypal heroes who sprang from the mixture of the two cultures that Gonzales used was counterbalanced with an approach that utilized more contemporary heroes from urban settings. The *pachuco* was one such hero. Distinguishing himself with a style of clothes that came to be known as the "zoot suit," the *pachucos* received national attention during the World War II era. As result of yellow journalism inciting prejudice against the *pachucos*, the "zoot suit riots" occurred when U.S. servicemen stationed in Southern California openly attacked the *pachucos* in the streets of Los Angeles. The other distinguishing characteristic of the *pachucos* was their mixture of Spanish and English and their generally hybrid subculture. A good example of the presentation of the *pachuco* hero in literature that also incorporates this kind of blending of languages and popular culture is the poem "El Louie," by José Montoya.

As demands for this new literature arose, small presses organized and began to publish works by the new Chicano authors. While such authors as Tomás Rivera and Rolando Hinojosa continued to write in Spanish with a mind to maintaining the language, there was a shift to publishing books written in English. This shift was due, in part, to the acculturation of Mexican Americans into English-speaking schools, where textbooks in English were the norm and therefore required students to learn to read English. These readers then became the target literary and consumer audience for these small presses. This shift to English texts became more evident when Quinto Sol, the first major Mexican-American publishing house, made the decision to print Spanish texts in bilingual versions with English translations. Publishing texts written only in the original Spanish was economically unfeasible, given the lack of opportunities for review, distribution, and sales of Spanish-language materials in the American book industry.

In the area of children's literature, based upon a survey of Mexican-American children's literature by the Council on Interracial Books for Children, there were roughly only 200 books with Hispanic topics published in the United States between the years of 1940 to 1973 that could be classified as children's texts. In addition to this small number of books in a burgeoning children's book market, the content of the books contained stereotyping, inaccuracies, and omissions, and most of these books were not written by Mexican Americans but about them by Anglo-American authors. More recently, in the last decade (1990s) there has been an improvement in the quantity and quality of Mexican-American children's books. (Barrera & de Cortés, 1993).

A new trend in Mexican-American/Latino children's literature, reflected in books published in English, is *interlingual* writing. This is different from bilingual in that it blends rather than separates the two languages of English and Spanish. As you read *Trino's Choice,* as well as some of the other texts in the chapters of this book, you will find instances of interlingual writing. The interlingual use resembles a natural and authentic speech that occurs in many Hispanic communities, creating a natural flow and interplay between the two languages.

Some Mexican-American/Chicano(a) writers, such as Rudolfo Anaya, Sandra Cisneros, Judith Ortiz Cofer, Gloria Anzaldúa, and Pat Mora, who have written for a primarily adult audience in the past, have in the last decade begun to write for children. They, along with Gary Soto, Ofelia Dumas Lachtman, Diane Gonzales Bertrand and Floyd Martínez, to name a few, have contributed high quality children's and young adult literature.

## Reading and Responding to the Story

When Trino first meets Lisana, Janie, Albert, and Jimmy at Maggie's bookstore, he thinks that these "school types" are crazy because they want to spend time listening to a writer read his poetry. In fact, to Trino, poetry is really dumb because no one can understand it; anyway, it's just a bunch of "stupid rhymes or broken sentences." He sure isn't going to waste any time trying to figure it out, either. And that goes for reading books, too. In fact, there isn't really anything much that Trino is interested in. But, these attitudes begin to change after he meets poet Emilce Montoya. Montoya's poems seem to carry messages that speak directly to Trino.

To prepare students for the story, read aloud the poem on page 40. Then ask students these guiding questions:

- What do you think the poet is saying in the poem?
- What life experiences might the poet have had in order to write this poem?
- How might this poem relate to the main character of the story, Trino?

Students can record their responses in a journal so that after they read the book, they can compare these initial responses to those they may have after the reading.

As the story progresses, Trino's life continues to change. One way for a reader to become involved in the author's development of this character is to keep a response journal in the form of a *diary* written from Trino's perspective. After reading each chapter, think about the events and interactions with the other characters from Trino's point of view. In other words, put yourself in Trino's shoes and ask yourself these questions: How did the events and conversations with the other characters in the chapter make you feel? How do these feelings affect your relationships with the other people in your life? What questions do these feelings raise for you? Diary entries can also be written from the other characters' perspectives, recording what they think about the changes they see occurring in Trino. For example, you might take the point of view of either Zipper or Rogelio, Trino's old friends.

One of the themes in this book is the power of words—reading words, understanding their many meanings, expressing your emotions and who you are through words, learning through words, using words as agents of change. The genre of poetry plays an important role in the story. At the poetry reading, Lisana asks Montoya the question, "Do you think anyone can write poetry?" Montoya answers, if you know how to feel, then you can write poetry, because poetry is about feelings. Maybe this answer is one of the reasons that the author chose poetry as a genre that can be both a way to discover the power that is in words and a means to create powerful messages through writing poems.

The power of poetry as an expressive genre may lie in the

usage of a small amount of words carefully chosen for their imagery, symbolism, rhythm, and resonance. I often think of poetry as condensed and concentrated thoughts and ideas that capture the essence of the phenomena that are part of our human existence. Through this distilled and potent solution of words, poetry presents our struggles, defeats, hopes, and joys, the emotions that bind us in our humanity. Perhaps the power of poetry lies in giving these human conditions a voice that presents multiple layers of meaning in just a few words. In doing so, all the meanings are preserved in a small, compact package, the contents of which can unwrap our memories and enfold new ones. In this package, we can carry with us these moments on our journey of knowing who we are, where we have come from, and where we are going.

## Building a Poet's Toolkit

The building blocks of poetry are words, just like any other genre. However, the way the poet combines these words is what makes poetry unique. The poet brings to the foreground certain elements of language when creating a poem. Two key elements are sound and rhythm. Using the sound inherent in words themselves, the poet combines these words into phrases that contain an almost musical quality. The rhythm of a poem usually refers to a pattern of sound created through a combination of words that gives the feeling of an underlying beat. Now, this does not necessarily mean that the beat has to be a regular beat—something you can tap your foot to. Free verse, for example, does not have a regular beat or meter, yet there is a movement and flow to the words reflecting natural patterns and rhythms of speech.

There are many kinds of poems. Some poems rhyme, and some have no rhyming words at all. There are poems that have a strong steady rhythm, but many defy finding a beat. There is even a unique type of poem that combines the visual with language content—*concrete poetry*—so that the words are arranged on the page to represent a visual image of the subject of the poem. A good way to introduce poetry writing to beginning poets is through formula poetry. These poems are created through following a prescribed, step-by-step formula, like the *biopoem* in Chapter 2. Formula poetry can also be used to teach various elements of language, such as syllabification, parts of speech, and figurative language. For example, the *haiku* and *cinquain* are two types of poems that are composed of a pattern of syllables. The American haiku, which was adapted from the Japanese form, is composed of three lines with five, seven, and five syllables, generally written about the seasons of the year—fall, winter, spring, summer—or some natural phenomenon, such as rain, wind, the ocean waves, and so on. Similarly, the cinquain, developed by Adelaide Crapsey in the early 1900s, follows a strict syllabic pattern; it was influenced by the Japanese poetry forms of haiku and tanka. From the French word for five, *cinq,* the five-line poem consists of two syllables, four syllables, six syllables, eight syllables, and two syllables.

The *diamante* is a seven-line, diamond-shaped poem that follows a pattern using parts of speech to describe opposite concepts or ideas. The first and seventh lines of the poem are single nouns that are opposites—for example, winter and summer. The second line consists of two adjectives that describe the first noun. The third line uses three gerunds (verb with an *–ing* ending) that relate to the first noun. The fourth line is a transition line that consists of four nouns—two that relate to the first noun, followed by two that relate to the opposite noun in the last line. The fifth line is like the third, but the gerunds relate to the last noun. The sixth uses two adjectives to describe the last noun. For example,

Winter

Snowy, cold

Sledding, snowboarding, ice-skating

Blizzards, snow-days, heat waves, vacation

Hiking, swimming, cycling

Hot, sunshine

Summer

## Developing Imagery and Figurative Language

One type of formula poem that works particularly well for helping writers develop their understanding and use of imagery or figurative language is the *sense poem.* The sense poem is a good way to teach students to write a simile. Through use of sensory language, the writer can remind readers and listeners of those concrete experiences that are attached to real events in their lives—those events experienced through the five senses. To help develop the use of sensory language in student writing, I usually begin with a brainstorming session about words or phrases that we associate with the different senses. Using a semantic web, I write *Sensory language* in the center circle, then the five sense words in connecting circles. Now, brainstorm words or phrases that relate to phenomena in these sensory ways. Here is an example:

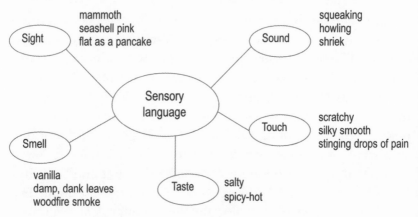

**Figure 5-1.** Map of Sensory Language

As you read *Trino's Choice,* note the author's use of sensory language, and choose examples that are particularly effective or meaningful for you. You can either record the examples in a reading response journal, or for a different approach, try using sticky notes in five different colors—one for each of the senses. Write the words that relate to the particular sense on the designated color and attach it to the edge of the page so that you can refer to it in your discussions and as a resource for your writing. Sometimes, words can evoke two senses at once. For example, in Chapter 1, page 5, Trino touches and feels the "hard cold egg and icy soda," and in the next sentence, he tastes "the cool, wet feel of them, especially with his mouth tasting dust."

## Writing Sense Poems

A *sense poem* is a five-line poem, with one line for each of the five senses: sight, hearing, smell, taste, and touch. Each line begins with the *subject* followed by *looks like, sounds like, smells like, tastes like,* and *feels like.* The poet fills in a word or phrase that creates a sensory image of the subject being described. Because of their use of "like," writing sense poems can help students recognize similes as they read poetry and incorporate similes in writing their own poetry. Sense poems also help to develop new ways of thinking about ordinary phenomena that occur in our daily lives by viewing those everyday occurrences and common objects in new and different ways.

When teaching students how to write sense poems, I start by asking them to list as many words or phrases that complete the prompt "Poetry feels like…" I begin with this sense because it can have a dual meaning: one that draws from the physical sense of touch as well as the sense of feeling brought on by emotions. Using this prompt first can also help students make the connection to the story. Do you remember Montoya's response to Lisana's question about writing poetry? Poetry is about feeling. I have used this brainstorming prompt many times, and often students begin with very concrete ideas that relate directly to elements of poetry or language. For example, typical initial responses are, "feels like rhyming," or "feels like hard words." In order to get students to think more creatively and beyond the familiar, I may ask students to expand their idea. For example, I ask them to describe what rhyming feels like: Say a few rhyming words. How do the words feel in your mouth? Usually, as students begin to experiment with different ways to think about how poetry feels, their responses naturally evolve as they build on each other's ideas. After a class brainstorming session, responses typically become less dependent on common associations and begin to incorporate sensory imagery that departs from the familiar and includes action. For example, "Poetry feels like crunchy peanut butter stuck on the roof of my mouth," and "Poetry feels like red-hot chiles dancing on my tongue," and "Poetry feels like sharp, stinging arrows that pierce my skin," all convey the sense of feeling with an action attached to it. The last example expresses a double meaning: physical touch, "stinging arrows piercing skin," and an implied emotional feeling attached to the stinging words that penetrate the skin and find their way into the soul. You can complete the sense poem about poetry by adding the other lines—looks, sounds, tastes, and smells like. Students can then write their own sense poems on the subject of their choice.

## Metaphor

A natural progression from the simile is learning about metaphor and how to incorporate metaphor into writing. Like simile, metaphor compares an object or idea to another object or idea. However, simile is an explicit comparison, using *like* or *as*, and metaphor is more implicit, and the *like* or *as* is omitted. In metaphor, the two things compared are often very different. For example, "clouds were slabs of dark gray marble" contrasts the common image of a light, airy, vaporous cloud to a heavy, dense and dark stone slab. Writing metaphors can sometimes be very difficult for students. As teachers, we often try to explain the concept of metaphor from our own experiences with various phenomena. This often results in confusion on the part of the student and results in a contrived metaphor that the student does not understand. To bring metaphor into the students' realm of understanding, I ask them to think of comparisons that have some relationship to the experiences in their daily lives. For example, I ask what are some activities that they do on a regular basis—swimming, going to a basketball game, walking in the woods, shopping at the mall. Events and objects that are part of these activities can provide ideas for comparisons. A metaphor that is based on personal experience will have more meaning for the student, and she or he will understand the comparison because it is based on personal knowledge about each object or idea. For example, one student, who played a lot of basketball, compared the sun to a round orange ball passing through the hoop. In the story, the author compares the sun to "an old bruise on the horizon" (p. 15). This is effective because it is an experience we all share. What colors do you see? Another example of metaphor in the story occurs in Montoya's poem about words. The metaphor occurs in the last line of the poem, "our words are hollow markings" (p. 38). A good guiding question might be, from what life experience of Montoya is this comparison drawn, and why are the words described as hollow markings?

## Publishing and Reading Poetry

After reading the book, students can write poems in response to the story using the diary entries they recorded from the point of view of Trino, using one of the formula poetry formats. The *diamante* might be an effective way to illustrate the opposing choices that Trino had to make in the story. Students could also choose to interpret their responses in free verse. They can also choose an event or other character to write a poem about. Or, they may want to write a poem about their personal reaction to the story. The process of writing poetry is similar to any other kind of writing—drafting, revising, editing, and publishing. If you already use the writing workshop approach in your classroom, this activity will fit into your writing time. In addition to drafting, revising and editing, you might want to add a self/peer reviewer/teacher assessment checklist for correct format of the formula poem (number of syllables, parts of speech, lines, etc.).

The poems can then be published in a class *anthology*. Students can also publish their own *chapbook* of poems. A poetry chapbook is a small collection of poems (generally not exceeding thirty-two pages). The chapbook got its name from peddlers called *chapmen* who sold small books (between thirty-two and sixty-four pages) as early as the sixteenth century. Containing mainly traditional literature, such as epics, legends, and folktales, chapbooks were printed on cheap paper so that they could be made accessible to the common people. Prior to the chapbook, books were primarily bought and read by the wealthy ruling class. Publishing is an important part of the writing process, and it also provides a way to assess student learning authentically.

Whether you choose to publish a class anthology or individual chapbooks, it is important to provide opportunities for students to read their poetry aloud, either to a small informal group or large audience in the context of a formal poetry reading, similar to the one in the story.

Reading poetry aloud is a performance and does take practice. Above all, the most important element for a reader to convey to the audience is the meaning of the poem. This requires attention to the phrasing of the words that create a unit of meaning. Often these phrases spill over from one line into the next, and a good reader will carry the phrase to its meaningful resting place. Commas mark many phrases. However, in some cases the only indicator of a unit of meaning is the way the words are arranged. The best way to discover these meaning units is to read the poem aloud several times. Another important element in a good performance is the inclusion of different dramatic vocal effects— whispering, speaking loudly, elongating syllables, and using a high- or low-pitched voice, emphasizing certain consonants or vowels. It is also important to speak at a pace that is not too fast and pronounce words distinctly so they can be understood. The point is to enhance the meaning, not detract from it.

As an extension to reading *Trino's Choice,* introduce and read poetry by other Latino/Latina poets, such as Judith Ortiz Cofer, José Martí, Pat Mora, Tomás Rivera, to name a few. One of my favorite sets of poems for young adult readers is Pat Mora's collection titled

*My Own True Name.* If you are planning a formal poetry reading as a culminating event to your study of the book, include poems by published authors. This is a way to involve those students who may not want to read their own poems in front of an audience. These poems can be individually read or performed as choral poetry read by two or more students. You may also want to include an introduction to the poetry reading that summarizes *Trino's Choice* and provides the audience with background knowledge of the story and insight on one of the book's underlying themes: the power of words.

## Working with Words

*Trino's Choice* is a book about words and poetry, and about the power that lies within both. In the book, the character of Montoya knows this power of words. After reading one of his poems, he chants, "la palabra, la palabra, the word, the word" (p. 38). Poetry is a genre that is created from the careful selection of words that evoke sensory images and emotions. Descriptive language is a tool for poets, just like it is for writers of creative prose. So, what makes poetry different? We know that a poem does not have to rhyme to be called poetry. But, poems do rely heavily on the auditory nature of words—the rhythm and sounds that make up individual words and the combinations of these words into phrases. This auditory element of poetry no doubt stems from its origins in the oral tradition. There is also a strong connection to musicality, perhaps reflecting the times when minstrels traveled from village to village, singing their poetry or when poetry was sung as part of religious rituals. Poetry also relies on condensed, compacted thought—economy of words to express a holistic impression. The following activities are designed to help you become more aware of the imagery, rhythm, and musicality that are inherent in the building blocks of poetry, *las palabras*, the words, and discover the different layers of meaning that words possess.

## Sound Bytes

Have you ever heard a word that you immediately liked

because of the way it sounded? This may *sound* silly, but if you think about it, there are words that just seem to roll out of your mouth and have a rhythmic flow and melodic quality that kind of rings in the air after you say them. I keep a collection of these in a little notebook, set aside just for these kinds of words. I titled my notebook *Sound Bytes*. Sometimes I even carry around a small tape recorder so that when I hear a word for my collection, I record it. Words are everywhere, so the collection sites are endless—on the radio in my car, at home watching television, in the movie theatre, even at the mall. Some of my favorite sounding words in English are *willowy, meander, cacophonous, slither*. To me, they are musical and rhythmic.

To begin the process of collecting your own sound bytes, brainstorm words that you think are rhythmic and melodious— words you like the sound of. Use these words as a beginning list for a student brainstorming session. Write the words on the board or overhead, and say them aloud to the class. Then ask for their contributions of words. Saying words aloud can stimulate interest and generate more thinking about words in this auditory way. As the words are said, write them down on an overhead, board, or chart paper. The next step in the process is to talk about each word (pick about five words from your list) to determine the meaning and the way it is used—to show action, to describe, to name something. Obviously, these are broad categories of parts of speech, but rather than identifying them as nouns, adjectives, and so on, the primary goal is knowing the general way in which these words can be used. As you discuss the meaning and usage, write these down and ask students to write the same information on an index card. On the front of the index card, write the word. On the back of the card, write the way it can be used and what it means. For example, *meander* can be used to show *action*, when it is used as meaning a kind of leisurely stroll that follows an indirect path. It can also be used to *name* that stroll or walk, and sometimes to name a bend in a river. Leave room to write additional meanings generated through other discussions about the word or by looking it up in a dictionary. Ask each student to choose at least five additional words and write the word and information in the same way on index cards. These can either be from the master list you generated as a group, or they can be new ones students choose on their own. It is a good idea to have students work in pairs. Talking about words, just as you modeled in the large group, is a way to help clarify the meaning of a word. Discussion can also serve as a kind of verbal revising and editing process before the meaning is written down. Now, ask students to look at their words and try pairing or grouping words together to create an image. These do not have to be complete sentences. The idea is to capture an impression. For example, looking at my list, I could pair *willowy* and *meander*. A completely different impression is created if I pair *cacophonous* with *meander*. Different pairings of words can help students recognize the variety of meanings that can be produced by the arrangement of words, an important tool for the poet.

Keep collecting *sound bytes* either as a class or individually. I like to keep a class collection as a resource for writing. For a class set, sort the words into the general categories—action, name, describing—and bind them with a ring binder. Students can keep adding to the words as they collect more sound bytes. Words can also be alphabetized so that students can easily incorporate *alliteration*, an auditory-based technique, into their poetry—*languid, lazy, leisurely days*. Another sound-based technique is *onomatopoeia*, those words that sound like what they mean—*splashes, crunch, buzz, whoosh*. Now those are words you can sink your ears into. And, they are fun to say. Maybe there are some examples in your collection already.

## Connecting across the Curriculum

In *Trino's Choice*, the main character, Trino, is faced with many choices that carry with them consequences that can affect his future. One of these choices involves which set of friends to hang out with. Trino is torn between his old friends, Zipper and Rogelio, and his new friends, Lisana, Hector, Jimmy, Albert, and Janie. Trino must also make a tough decision about joining Rosca's group. To Lisana and her friends, Rosca and his friends are bad news. To Zipper and Rogelio, and even Trino, Lisana and her friends are labeled "the school types." In every school, there are a number of different kinds of groups that could be considered microcultures that are part of the overall culture of school. Many groups in schools are also defined by participation in some school activity. For example, typical school-based groups are athletes, cheerleaders, musicians, the drama group or some other school club, and those who make good grades and are always on the honor roll. There are also other groups that may be based in com-monality of gender, ethnicity, or language. For example, students who are newly immigrated to this country and speak another lan-guage other than English as their first language may socialize together at school, eat lunch together, and sit together in class as a way of supporting one another in a new environment while learning a new language. Most people belong to more than one cultural group both in and outside the school setting. Sometimes, as in the case of Trino, membership in one group may come into conflict with belonging to another group. Can you identify the dif-ferent microcultures in your school? What determines member-ship in a certain group? In what kinds of typical activities are group members involved? *Ethnography*, which has its roots in *anthropology*, comes from the Greek *ethnos*, which denotes a people in a race or cultural group. A person who studies culture and describes the lives of people within a specific cultural group is called an *ethnog-rapher*. The following activities are designed to involve students in becoming ethnographers of their school and community.

## Studying Your School and Community through Ethnographic Inquiry

One of the first things an ethnographer does as she or he enters the *field*, which is the term for the physical location for the study, is to draw a site map. You may have already drawn a site map of a particular space or room in Chapter 2. The site map of a school and surrounding community is similar, but, it focuses on a larger area, indicating the locations of the school buildings, athletic fields, major streets, houses, stores, parks, or any other physical features in close proximity to the school. As a kind of predrawing activity, take a walk around the school grounds with your class and note the various physical features and their relationship to each other. You may even want to have students take some observational notes or draw some preliminary sketches. You can also provide students with a template on which to record the placement of buildings and other features as you take your tour. To make a template, start with a city street map. Try to locate a map that is part of a city directory of neighborhood or community district maps. To create a template, first make a photocopy of the map. Depending on the map's size, you may want to enlarge your copy to allow for adding representations of the various features on your map. Using this copy, make an overhead transparency. This transparency can be used to construct a class version of the map of your school and community site map, using the information students collected on their tour of the school and community. Overlay a blank transparency page to draw in the various physical features. This allows for correcting any misplacement of features and also saves your original copy for future use. Provide students with another copy of the template so they can have a complete and accurate copy of the school and community. I have also done this activity in rural settings where there are no maps and the main street is a gravel road. If you live in a small rural setting, you can prepare a simple template or have students create their own. I often have a team of students enlarge the completed transparency to create a mural-sized map. Simply tape up craft paper on a wall and use the overhead projector to enlarge the image. Then, trace the images onto the paper section-by-section.

## Identifying the Microcultures in Your School Setting

Students usually share interests and participate in activities with more than one group or microculture that exists within the overall school culture. Everyone participates in being part of a class. Individual classrooms share a particular culture in which certain social norms are present. As a member of this classroom microculture, one needs to know and practice these norms, which include rules of behavior and may involve use of a specific discourse or ways of talking. These norms may be dictated by the content of the class itself. For example, a science classroom may have a different set of norms than a history class. There may be different rules of behavior involving safety in a science classroom that are not found in a history class. Also, the way you discuss science experiments is probably different from the way you talk about an historical event. There is also a different vocabulary associated with each discipline. The same is true of extracurricular activities-based groups. Think of the differences between being a member of the wrestling team and the chorus or the drama club. Not only do different rules of behavior apply when participating in each group, but each requires different physical movement and ways of communicating as well as different modes of dress. Membership in groups may also involve gender. These different identifying markers also apply to different social groups.

To identify the microcultures in your school, have each student list those groups to which they belong. Under each group heading, record some of the social norms associated with that group, such as appropriate or typical behavior within the group, some common group activities, and jargon, slang, or vocabulary that may be specific to the group. When students have completed their lists, compile a class list of the different groups. Ethnographers also use photographs as *data* to document their studies. If you have access to school cameras, students can take photographs of the different groups represented. Another source for photographs may be duplicate pictures from the school yearbook. To extend your discussion of *Trino's Choice,* ask students to think about the choices they have faced when being a member of one group has conflicted with belonging to another group. For example, consider these questions. What were some of the consequences involved? How was a decision reached?

## Locating Community-Based Activities

In *Trino's Choice,* Lisana and her friends frequently went to the local bookstore to buy books and attend the poetry and book readings Maggie arranged for the community. What are some of the resources for teens in your local community? Refer to your school and community map. Are there any places, such as a bookstore, a Y.M.C.A., Boys and Girls Club, swimming pool, or park, that are in close proximity to the school? What kinds of activities are offered to school-age students? Are there after-school programs? Students can collect informational brochures and add them to the *data set*—the information you collect in your study, such as site maps, descriptions of kinds of groups, photographs. Students can also prepare and conduct interviews of local business owners and directors of after-school programs. Compiling this kind of community information, along with the various school-based activities available to students, can provide them with good choices for where and how to spend their time both in and out of school. Presenting the information at a school open house, the Parent/Teacher Organization (PTO), or other community-based meetings, posting it on a class, school, or district website, or broadcasting it as a Public Service Announcement (PSA) on a local radio station moves the activity beyond the classroom into the larger public sphere and provides a valuable resource to the community.

## Summary

Generally speaking, knowing how to read and understand words in texts and learning how to use words to communicate effectively both orally and through writing are key to being a literate person in our society. In the context of school, there are various interpretations of literacy that reflect differing ideologies and pedagogical approaches. For example, one approach to literacy focuses on explicit instruction in decoding words and views comprehension as a set of skills that leads to knowledge of vocabulary and the ability to answer specific questions directly related to the text (Myers, 1996). Another approach recognizes the role of the reader as an active agent who brings her or his background knowledge and life experiences to the complex processes of reading and writing. This emphasis on process is found in the reading and writing workshop approach popular in many elementary and middle-school classrooms (Atwell, 1998; Calkins, 1994). In *Trino's Choice*, Montoya talks about literacy and what it means for him. Reading is not just figuring out letters and sounds, but also means getting "into the words" to "figure out what they're saying to you" (p. 46). Thus, he extends the notion of literacy beyond decoding words and extends comprehension as answering specific textually related questions to include making meaning that is relevant to the reader's life experience. However, Montoya's definition does not stop there. He also speaks about the power that reading and understanding words gives. Without that power, "people can tell you what you ought to think" (p. 47). With that power, "nobody'll ever take what's yours out of your hands," and you will be able "to protect what you love most" (p. 47). Through the power of words, you gain the ability to transform yourself through critical reflection and action, what Freire (1972) calls *praxis*, and to engender positive social change. This kind of literacy, *critical literacy*, is based on the interrogation of the historical, political, and social position of text, author, and reader for the purpose of generating positive social action. Critical literacy reaches beyond the schoolhouse door into all aspects of daily life and transforms and empowers the reader to read the word and the world (Freire, Macedo, 1987). This power begins with knowing the power of words. It is what Montoya means when he says, "la palabra, la palabra."

# Chapter 6

## *Spirits of the High Mesa:*
## In the Name of Progress

### Story Summary

*Spirits of the High Mesa* is a story about change—change that is imposed on people in the name of "progress." This kind of change can sometimes be a double-edged sword. One edge carves a path lined with modern conveniences, making life easier and opening up new ways of thinking. The sword's other edge may cut away the long-standing traditions and ways of knowing that are also tied to one's cultural identity. At the beginning of the story, we meet Flavio, a young Mexican-American boy who is pretty content with his life. Flavio spends his time going to school, listening to radio shows such as *The Shadow* and *Fibber McGee and Molly*, and doing his ranch chores alongside his grandfather, El Grande. The small, rural town of Capulin, New Mexico, where Flavio and his family live, has no hotel, no police, and no electricity. But, that is about to change. When the Rural Electrification Administration (REA) comes to Capulin and shows a movie about the "miracle of electricity," some of the people, mainly the women of the village, agree that it will make life much easier. For El Grande, however, the coming of electricity does not mean *progreso*, or progress. Instead, he warns the villagers that they are losing respect for the land. "Our children will not have the same peace we have known," he says, referring to the *atómica*, the atomic bomb that was rumored to have been constructed just over the mountain at Los

Alamos. For El Grande, the changes that will come with the electricity will push them further away from the teachings of their
forefathers. But, El Grande, in his wisdom, knows that one cannot
stop *progreso.* The power lines go up and the light bulbs glow,
refrigerators hum, ice cream is sold at the store run by Flavio's
mother, and tortillas are replaced with toasted bread. Even when
the men of the village surrender to their wives in the war against
progress, El Grande will have nothing to do with electricity, and
he maintains a silent protest against the R.E.A., the *molino,* and
even the U.S. Forest Service *(floresta).*

Just as El Grande predicted, along with the electricity come
other changes. The logging company and sawmill *(molino)* brings
*gringo* workers and their families to Capulin. For Flavio and the
other Mexican-American children, this means a big change at
school. Before the gringo kids arrive, Mrs. Majors devotes herself
to teaching Flavio and his friends all she knows—reading, writing,
math. But, after the gringo kids come, they seem to get all the
attention. She calls on them for answers, lets them do the fun
chores. She even makes the Mexican-American kids change their
names so the gringos can say them—Timoteo becomes Tim, Fed-
erico is called Fred. This *Americanization* of Spanish names continues to be an issue today. You may remember that in Chapter 3
(*Call Me Consuelo*), Consuelo wants to be called by her real name
rather than Connie, the Americanized version her grandmother
uses. Then suddenly, one day Mrs. Majors makes it a rule that no
one can speak Spanish in the schoolyard. Spurred on by the new
Americanization and English-only policies and the privileging of
the Anglo students by Mrs. Majors, fights break out between the
gringo kids and the Mexican-American kids.

More and more gringo families move in and tensions
increase, until one night, a gringo worker is found dead. This
event shakes the little town, and the once quiet village changes
dramatically. El Grande, who had once been the law in the town,
begins to withdraw and spend more time alone on his upper
mountain ranch. Even the village men, who once were so

adamantly against *progreso,* take jobs as loggers and workers at the *molino.* Some even go to work in Duke City. Progress has brought change, and Flavio is faced with coming to grips with this new world. Even within his own family, perspectives on change or progress differ. Flavio is torn between his father's view of the world, in which "education is the only thing that counts in life," and El Grande's view, "working the land with your bare hands and not depending on any other man for anything," was the only way to live your life.

Finally, Flavio and his family, without El Grande, move to Duke City. El Grande chooses to stay in Capulin. Flavio's new city life is filled with football practice, homework, television, and new friends. When news of El Grande's death comes, Flavio is at first very angry that El Grande has left him. But, he soon realizes that El Grande had done what he said he would do, "die with dignity and honor." El Grande had gone to be with his mountain and his old friends, the ancient Indian spirits, in a place that was far better than anything in his changed world.

At the end of the story, Flavio, a man recovering from cancer and dealing with chemotherapy, returns to Capulin, to El Grande's mountain. Here he relives his memories of his time with El Grande. He recalls the times when he went to baseball games instead of spending time with El Grande learning about the sacred slopes of the Pedernal. But, returning to the place of his youth, Flavio sees the vision that El Grande had seen, and he is once again connected to the wisdom and power that had been a part of his life before the *progreso* came to Capulin.

## Building Background Before You Read

The setting of the story, the state of New Mexico, has a history that is similar to other states, such as Texas, California, Florida, and the countries of Mexico, Central America, and the Caribbean islands. All contain the common thread of indigenous cultures colliding with the conquest and colonization by Spain stemming from the arrival of Columbus to the "new world." The rich cultural history of New Mexico's people is depicted by the symbols on the state flag. The red Zia Sun, which originated with the ancient Zia Pueblo Indians, consists of a circle representing life and love that has no beginning and no end. The four straight lines that radiate outward from the circle reflect the belief in the sacredness of the number four—the seasons of spring, summer, fall, winter; directions of north, west, south, east; segments of day, dawn, noon, dusk, midnight; and the cycle of life in childhood, youth, adulthood, and old age—and the spiritual beliefs of harmony among all things in the universe. This Zia Sun symbol is placed on a background of Spanish gold. The historical narrative of the land and the people of New Mexico can be divided into four periods. The first begins with settlement by highly developed indigenous populations. The second period is marked by the arrival of the Spanish in 1598 (in reality, much of the colonization was affected by peoples of mixed Spanish, Indian, and African heritage), bringing the familiar cycle of conquest and colonization. The third period may be defined by an independence from Spain, the transition to Mexican government and later the status of a U.S. territory after the United States and Mexican War. The fourth and final period begins with statehood.

The first peoples to settle what is now New Mexico were thought to be the Folsom, who inhabited much of the Southwest at the end of the Ice Age, between 9000 and 8000 B.C. Sometime after 300 A.D., the Mogollon Mimbres people inhabited southwestern New Mexico and eastern Arizona. The Mimbres culture is best known for its highly artistic black-on-white pottery that was decorated with geometric and naturalistic designs. The Mimbres first lived in subterranean pithouses that were entered through the roof. Later the Mimbres lived in dwellings called *pueblos,* which is the Spanish word for towns or villages. This name for the people who lived in these permanent dwellings was given by Spanish explorer Francisco Vásquez de Coronado when he traveled through the region in 1540; *pueblos* was used to distinguish them from the more nomadic Apache and Navajo.

The Anasazi are perhaps the most well known of the ancient civilizations of the Southwest. Their stone houses and cliff dwellings and artifacts can be found today in areas reaching from southwestern Colorado and Utah to northeastern Arizona and northwestern New Mexico. The Anasazi evolved from a hunting and gathering society to an agricultural one, much like their neighbors the Mogollon. They are best known for their architectural stone and adobe structures, which are evidences of their highly developed skills as masons. At the height of their culture, which was between 700 and 1300 A.D., they built and populated large, multistoried cliff dwellings with plazas and *kivas*. The Anasazi, like the Mogollon, began to decline after 1300 A.D. and by 1600 A.D. they had abandoned the area. Various theories have developed about their mysterious disappearance from the region. The most substantiated are connected to the depletion of natural resources, particularly water, coupled with population increases and a breakdown of the social structure.

Later arrivals to the area were Athabascan people. Anthropologists believe that these early people migrated from Asia, crossing Beringia into what is now Alaska and western Canada. The Athabascan people do not believe this; they believe they were always on this continent. These early people are now known as Ingalik, Koyukon, Tanana, Holikachuk, Gwich'in, Han, Upper Tanana, Ahtna, and Tanaina. "The People" or Dine'e, now called Navajo, and the Jicarilla Apache split off from the Athabascan peoples, who remained in the northern regions and migrated to what is now New Mexico between 1300 and 1500 A.D. The distinction between these two Athabascan groups is generally based on lifestyle and means of survival. The Navajo, who lived in *hogans*, were farmers and herders. They adapted to the coming of the Spaniards by using the wool from Spanish sheep to weave clothes, blankets, and rugs and made this an important part of their culture. This art continues to be a part of their culture today. The Jicarilla Apache (Jicarilla means *little basketmakers*) were primarily hunters and gatherers.

The Spanish began arriving in the Southwest in the 1500s. In the 1530s, on his trek from what was believed to have been Galveston, Texas, to Mexico, Álvar Núñez Cabeza de Vaca crossed southern New Mexico and began telling the tale of the Seven Cities of Cíbola. Cabeza de Vaca was followed by Spanish conquistadors, such as Coronado, who were lured by the tale of the cities of gold. In 1598, Juan de Oñate arrived at Caypa, a Pueblo village at the confluence of the Río Chama and Río Grande, with his soldiers, colonists, and livestock. He established the first Spanish capital near what is now Espanola, New Mexico. This territory of Spain had its next two centuries marked by colonization, as well as Indian revolts against the Spanish. In 1812, Mexico declared its independence from Spain and won its independence in 1821. New Mexico had passed from New Spain to Mexico. However, after the Mexican-American War in 1848, New Mexico was annexed to the United States. In 1850, New Mexico, which included present-day Arizona, southern Colorado, southern Utah, and southern Nevada, was designated a U.S. territory. In 1863, New Mexico was divided in half, and the Territory of Arizona was created. In the next three decades, New Mexico witnessed the bloodshed of the famous Lincoln County Wars. The "Wars," set into motion by competing rings attempting to dominate lands and natural resources, were characterized by lawlessness that broke out between two factions of civilian merchants and cattlemen, involving gunfights, murders, and cattle rustlings. On one side was the infamous William H. Bonney, alias "Billy the Kid," who was shot by Sheriff Pat Garrett in Fort Sumner, New Mexico, in 1881. Bonney sided with and helped to protect the lands of the native *hispanos* of New Mexico from encroachment by migrants from the eastern United States. In 1886, the famous Apache leader Geronimo surrendered, ushering in a new era in New Mexico history in which conflict with the Indians ceased. Only after Anglo migrants formed a majority population in New Mexico did Congress admit New Mexico to the Union as the 47th state, in 1912.

## The New State and the New Deal

At the beginning of the story, the little town of Capulin, New Mexico, is without many of the modern conveniences, such as indoor plumbing, running water, and electric power, that the more urban areas take for granted as a way of life. In the early 1900s, electricity was considered a luxury for most households and was available only in large urban areas of the country. As late as the mid-1930s, most rural homes were without electricity, just like those in the town of Capulin. Cows were milked by hand, women cooked on woodstoves and washed clothes with a scrub-board in a tub of water that they pumped by hand from a well and carried to the house. Food was preserved by canning or kept cool for a time in a "root cellar." Kerosene lanterns lighted homes, barns, general stores, other small-town businesses, and schools. Then, in 1935, Franklin D. Roosevelt established the Rural Electrification Administration (REA), and in 1936, Congress passed the Rural Electrification Act. Through the REA, federal loans for constructing electric power lines throughout rural areas in the United States were made available. The REA was built on the belief that bringing affordable electricity to rural areas would elevate the standard of living and increase the economic competitiveness and stability for small family farms and thus halt the flight of the rural farmer to the larger urban areas. However, rural electrification did not halt the migration to urban areas, and as time passed, the number of small family-run farms declined. This trend is an important theme in *Spirits of the High Mesa,* and at the end of the story, we find Flavio and his family well integrated into the urban lifestyle.

## Los Alamos and the Nuclear Era

The issue of the use of atomic energy for nuclear warfare is briefly introduced at the beginning of *Spirits of the High Mesa, when* El Grande refers to the rumors that the *atómica* (atom bomb) used in the destruction of Hiroshima and Nagasaki was built just over the mountains from Capulin in Los Alamos. Then, at the end of the story, a connection between nuclear testing and cases of cancer in humans is implied, as we find Flavio, the adult, undergoing chemotherapy treatments. Thus, even though it plays an understated role in the plot of the story, the controversy over the use of nuclear weapons and their negative effects is implicitly connected to the idea that not all change is for the good. With "progress" comes consequence and, sometimes, loss of innocence.

At the time of the establishment of Los Alamos as a nuclear weapons laboratory, the United States was fully entrenched in the war against Germany and Japan. In both arenas the outcome of the war was filled with uncertainty, and the possibility of a long involvement with heavy casualties became an ever-increasing reality. In the summer of 1942, the United States government brought together a group of scientists, led by J. Robert Oppenheimer, to discuss plans for designing and building a nuclear weapon to use against the enemies of the United States to bring an end to the war. The site for the creation of a nuclear laboratory, Los Alamos, New Mexico, was chosen after consideration of sites in California, Nevada, Utah, and Arizona. At the time of its selection, Los Alamos was home to Los Alamos Ranch School, a private boarding school that focused on outdoor education for boys from wealthy families. The geographic location of Los Alamos, with its controlled road access and surrounding canyons that would be suitable for explosives tests, as well as the existing school buildings that could be used for laboratories, made the site highly desirable. So, in December of 1942, what had previously been a school for boys, became a laboratory for nuclear arms in Los Alamos.

The detonation of the atomic bomb, called "Fat Man," at the Trinity site in the New Mexico desert, ushered in a new era that held the prospect of nuclear annihilation for everyone on the planet. In the 1950s, bomb shelters were built, even by private citizens, and school children went through drills in which everyone would get under their desks with their jackets or sweaters over their heads to protect them from flying glass. Of course, the reality of being at ground zero of an atomic blast makes the drills seem absurd and even surreal. When the Cuban Missile Crisis occurred in 1962, the threat of nuclear war and the destruction that would result became a reality for every citizen in the United States and the rest of the world. The end of the Cold War has moved us to a new era that has reduced the anxiety of nuclear warfare. Today, nuclear power is less thought of in terms of its destructive power and fear of impending doom, and more, some might argue, in terms of how it serves as a benefit to our lives. Approximately one-sixth of the world's electricity is generated by nuclear power, and more than five million cancer patients receive radiation therapy each year. Perhaps this is another revolution in the cycle of "progress."

## Reading and Responding to the Story

In my children's literature classes, as part of learning how to analyze and evaluate critically a piece of children's literature, we discuss the literary elements—plot, setting, characters, style, and theme. The importance of how all of the elements work together to create a good story is emphasized. Yet, time and again, the primacy of a good plot is raised in the discussions. The general argument is, "If the book doesn't have a good plot, students won't stay interested, and they probably won't want to finish it." When I think about how many books I have put away after reading a few chapters because I just couldn't force myself to continue to plow through them, I have to agree that without a good plot, centered in a believable conflict, it can be difficult, and maybe even impossible, to keep any reader engaged.

One important element of the plot is the *conflict*. The conflict provides the tension necessary to forward the action of a plot. There are four kinds of conflict played out in fictional stories: *person-against-nature, person-against-self, person-against-person, and person-against-society* (Tomlinson, Lynch-Brown, 2002). In young adult literature, person-against-nature is a type of conflict found in adventure and survival stories. In this kind of conflict, the main character has to overcome the physical forces of nature in order to survive. A person-against-person conflict usually centers in problems involving siblings or peers and sometimes adults. Person-against-self is a familiar conflict found in many coming-of-age stories. In this kind of conflict, the main character, or protagonist, is involved in a struggle with her or his own beliefs, values, and attitudes in terms of how they affect her or his personal ambitions or goals. In *Trino's Choice,* for example, Trino is faced with the inner struggle of personal values and moral choices that can potentially affect his future. In *Spirits of the High Mesa,* we find Flavio also struggling with choices that can affect his life, but in a different way. Whereas Trino's choice may determine whether he is heading toward a life of crime and prison, Flavio's choices reflect a tension between what he has learned from the culturally based teachings of El Grande and the new way of life that is being ushered in with new technologies. This leads to the final conflict.

The person-against-society is found in many young adult stories. In this kind of conflict, issues such as the destruction and/or conservation of the environment, civil rights, and political upheaval that may result from war are raised. In the story of *Spirits,* both Flavio and his grandfather, El Grande, are brought face-to-face with the environmental impact brought about by a modern technology that not only changes the physical landscape in and around their village, but also shapes the cultural landscape away from their traditional way of life. This outer environmental conflict plays a primary role in setting up the inner conflict between the old cultural traditions and the new values brought about by a new way of life. Together they create a tension that helps to forward the movement of the plot. Thus, these interrelated conflicts, working in tandem with strong character development, are the two literary elements that are emphasized in the following activities.

## Plotting the Plot

There are different kinds of plot structures, but the most common type develops chronologically, relating the events in the order they occur over the period of time of the story. Generally, in this kind of dramatic plot, the setting is established, the characters are introduced, and the conflict is stated in the opening chapters. After this *exposition*, the plot is advanced in a series of events that build to a climax that leads to a solution of the problem and a conclusion or *denouement* of the story. In the *episodic* plot, which is a variation of a chronological plot, each chapter is self-contained with its own conflict and resolution. The maintenance of the same setting and characters in each of the episodes serves to unify the overall story. Sometimes the technique of *flashback* is used in the development of the plot. This technique disrupts the chronological order of events and allows the author to begin the story with the present action and later introduce the reader to events that occurred earlier in time.

In the book *Spirits of the High Mesa*, Floyd Martínez forwards his dramatic plot chronologically and ends the book with a *coda*. A coda is a section added at the end of a literary work that is not necessary to the plot structure, but provides the reader with additional information. It is similar to its musical counterpart of the same name, and is usually added for dramatic effect. In the coda to *Spirits*, Flavio is portrayed as an adult returning to Capulin in search of his cultural and spiritual roots.

One strategy to help students follow the development of the plot while reading the story is to construct a graphic organizer that illustrates the exposition, the rising action, the climax, the denouement, and the end of the story, including a coda if there is one. Details summarizing events that occur in each section can be recorded chronologically chapter by chapter. This graphic can be created as a whole class project, in literature circles, or by individual students. The first step is to draw the basic plot line, labeling each of the sections. See Figure 6.1.

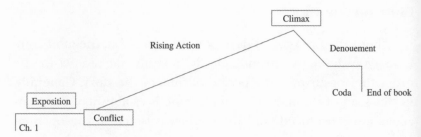

**Figure 6-1.** Basic Plot Development

Next, students must identify and outline the exposition chapters, and outline the chapter in which the conflict is first introduced. See Figure 6.2.

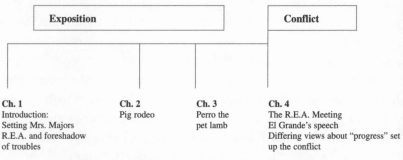

**Figure 6-2.** Plotting the Exposition and Conflict

Students then continue to outline the primary events for chapters leading up to the climax and the subsequent chapters of the denouement and coda. Students can also include the author's subheadings by dividing the book into three parts: *Parte Una,* Beginnings (Chapters 1–6), *Parte Dos,* Transitions (Chapters 7–18), and *Parte Tres,* Vision (Chapter 19) on the graphic outline. See Figure 6.3.

## Casting the Characters

The development of believable and memorable characters is

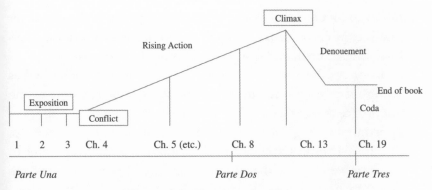

**Figure 6-3.** Plotting the Plot

also essential to any good plot. A strong, well-developed, or *round* character can become a friend with whom a reader can identify or a role model whom one can look up to and aspire to be like. That is not to say that the protagonist is a perfect character who always makes the right choices and never makes mistakes. The creation of round characters requires a portrayal of both the strengths and weaknesses that make up the human condition. In *Spirits of the High Mesa,* the character portrayals of Flavio and El Grande provide the reader with opportunities to engage with real people who are involved with struggles that are complex and not easy to resolve. Throughout the story's twists and turns, the characters develop and change or adjust to the new circumstances presented in the plot. In the case of *Spirits,* the change that the characters experience is tightly linked to the change that occurs when the newly introduced technologies and influx of people from a different culture clash with those who have spent their entire lives in Capulin, steeped in the cultural traditions and the ways of knowing of their ancestors.

Most fiction for children usually has one or two main characters, such as Flavio and El Grande, with several supporting or *secondary* characters. A secondary character is generally not as well developed as the protagonists. Development of secondary characters varies from story to story. Some may be described in more detail than others, depending on their roles in the conflict and the events of the plot. Sometimes the author may use a *flat* characterization to forward the plot or emphasize a point. A flat character usually exhibits one attribute such as greed, envy, truthfulness, wisdom, and so forth, and can sometimes be stereotypical.

In *Spirits,* Mrs. Majors, a secondary character, is described as having more than one attribute, and she exhibits change as the plot progresses. For example, when she first comes to Capulin, she is portrayed as "big, mean and red-faced, with a car-horn voice" (p. 11); she arrives in Capulin under curious circumstances. Later in the story, we discover that she is a dedicated teacher who is committed to helping her students to learn. But, when the *gringos* come to school, Mrs. Majors begins to change and starts to give them the "fun chores like passing out the singing books," while Flavio and his friends "got to carry wood" (p. 74).

So how do authors develop their characters? How do we get to know what they look like, what personality traits they exhibit, what they believe in and value? There are several ways we get to know characters in literature. For example, the author may tell us about a character:

- Through actions, habits, and patterns of behavior
- Through inner thoughts and motivations revealed either through a narrator or through first-person inner dialogue
- Through dialogue interactions with other characters
- Through what other characters say about him or her—his or her strengths, weaknesses, personality traits
- Through descriptions of his or her physical appearance

In the case of Mrs. Majors, in the first chapter of the book, we learn about what she looks and sounds like (physical descriptions), as well as the speculations about her past that might have brought her to Capulin (what others say). We relive the event at *la cuesta* that caused her to be brought to the village (actions), and we find out why she may have been persuaded to stay. We also hear her response (speech interactions) to Flavio's bell-ringing incident that tells us she is not a traditional type of teacher. From all of these events and types of information, then, we begin to form impressions of Mrs. Majors.

Just as students traced the development of the plot, a similar activity can help students identify whether the character is a main character, secondary character, round or flat, and the ways the author develops the character throughout the novel. While reading each chapter, use sticky notes to keep a record of the name of the character and the way the author reveals something about him or her, using a simple code that corresponds to the above list: A = actions, habits, patterns of behavior; T = thoughts and motivations; D = dialogue; OC = what other characters say; and P = physical appearance. After reading the chapter, create a three-column page similar to the one below. At the beginning of the book, you may only have enough information to fill in the first two columns. In the case of the character Flavio, however, readers may predict that he is a primary character because of his narrator stance. After reading the first chapter, the record might look like this.

| Uno—Chapter 1 | | |
|---|---|---|
| **Character's Name** | **Development—Ways of knowing** | **Type** |
| Flavio | Inner thoughts, dialogue, actions | Primary—protagonist |
| El Grande | What others say (Flavio as narrator), actions, speech | |
| Mrs. Majors | What others say, actions, dialogue, physical description | |
| Mother | Dialogue | |
| Father | What others say (Flavio) | |
| Emilio Sanchez | What others say (Flavio) | |
| Lorenzo | What others say (Flavio) physical description | |
| Jose Torres | | |
| Malvino | What others say (Flavio) | |
| Pedro | What others say (Flavio) | |
| Juan | What others say (Flavio) | |
| Dolores | What others say (Flavio) | |
| | What others say (Flavio) | |

**Figure 6-4.** Character Development

Students can also make predictions about the type of characters introduced in the first chapter. After reading more chapters, they can check their predictions and compare them to the actual development of the characters within the plot. Some characters in *Spirits* are introduced for the sole purpose of contributing to the action of the plot. After that job is done, they make an exit from the story and often do not appear again. For example, in Chapter 8, *Ocho,* when Flavio is expelled from school for fighting with Tusa, he goes to his mother's store. Enter the character Rumalda Ortiz, who is "old and had no teeth." Placing her in the store buying rubber boots saves Flavio from his mother's wrath and punishment, "at least for a little while" (p. 78). Through this brief introduction and description of a *flat* character, the plot is moved forward. Having done her job of providing a diversion to the expected response by Flavio's mother, *Doña* Rumalda exits from the story. Recording the characters and how they develop as they appear in each chapter can provide concrete examples for students to help build their understanding of ways an author develops the plot through various types of characters.

## El Grande

We learn about Don Ezequiel, or El Grande, through descriptions of his actions and what others, particularly Flavio, say and think about him. But, we also discover El Grande's deep-seated beliefs and values through his speech and communications with other characters. In many instances, in these interactions with others, we see El Grande as a wise teacher who, through his speech, passes down the cultural knowledge that has guided him and his ancestors in their ways of living in harmony with the environment. For example, when the new gringo kid whom Flavio and his friends nicknamed Tusa takes Lupita Apodaca's tortilla from her *lonche,* which results in a fight and Flavio's expulsion from school, Flavio has to tell El Grande what happened. Instead of using the *reata,* the "dreaded fine-leather whip," El Grande teaches Flavio about the meaning of hatred, fighting, and the different, kinds of power and control (p. 78). El Grande also uses examples from nature, such as the analogy of the chameleon (p. 101), to teach Flavio the importance of never losing one's identity even when one is forced to adapt to other environments. The use of symbolism also occurs when El Grande quotes verses from the Bible and sings his song *Cuatros Milpas*. In each of these examples, there are deeper meanings that Flavio must interpret and apply to his life.

As readers, we are involved in many levels of reading and interpreting the text. For example, El Grande's teachings not only have a certain meaning for the character of Flavio, but they also contain a meaning for the individual reader. Therefore, it is possible to construct different meanings from the same passage of text. One meaning can be constructed within the context of the story, using the events of the plot, the historical time, and physical setting in which the story takes place, and the life histories that are developed for each character. In other words, readers can construct a meaning that is situated within the plot. This is the meaning we try to access when we assess a student's comprehension of text, whether it is through retellings or other means. This kind of interpretation is similar to the way many dramatic actors approach a role or part in a play. They study the character's lines and how they interact with the other characters in the context of the plot, so they can learn how the character thinks and what her or his motivations are. This enables the actor to portray the character in such a believable way that the audience sees and hears only the character, not the actor. This is usually referred to as being and staying *in character.*

There are also other meanings that a reader constructs that take the story off the page and into the context of the reader's own life. An often-used instructional strategy for accessing students' interpretations of texts as they relate to their own life experiences is through reader response journals. There are also meanings that are constructed when we discuss a story with others. In such discussions, readers can present their interpretations through their own experiential perspectives. Through this social interaction the potential exists for a transformation of the individual reader's thinking about the text, which is built upon the combined readings and constructions of meanings of all the readers involved in the discussion about the text. The following activity, *Three Ways of Thinking About Text,* is designed to access the different ways students think about and create interpretations of the texts they are reading.

To begin the activity, locate and highlight, either with pencil or sticky notes, the passages in which El Grande speaks, imparting his wisdom and passing down cultural knowledge through his various examples to Flavio. Using the graphic organizer below, record the page number of the passage read. For example, one of the first passages in which we hear El Grande's teaching voice is on page 42 of the text, when he tells Flavio about his heritage. Next, think about how Flavio might interpret these words and record this under *Thinking in Character.* Read the passage again, thinking about the passage in terms of your life experience. There may be a person who is similar to El Grande, or you may remember a teaching example told to you by a family member or friend. Record your response under *Thinking off the Page.* Finally, with a buddy or in a small group, discuss the different meanings that each person has constructed and recorded under *Thinking off the Page.* After the discussion, record any new ideas or responses under *Thinking with Others.*

In a recent young adult literature class that I taught, I sat in on a discussion group of *Spirits.* Here is a page generated from reading the passage on page 129. See Figure 6.5.

## Developing a Critical Stance

Much of what El Grande teaches deals with how humans must learn to live together with each other as well as with other living things that inhabit the natural world. The key to living in harmony with one's environment is respect, and respect really rests on the question of control. El Grande might ask: Are you involved in

| Text Page | Thinking in Character | Thinking off the Page | Thinking with Others |
|---|---|---|---|
| P. 42 | I am part Indio and part Gachupin just like my grandparents. El Grande says this mixture of two peoples made them very wise and brave. I can see those things in El Grande. I want to be like him, so I am going to work hard like he says. | My grandmother always used to tell us about her grandmother who, during times of religious persecution, stood up for what she believed in and was actually put in prison for her beliefs. It made me wonder how strong I would be under similar circumstances. But, maybe I get my bulldog tenacity from a long line of strong women. | Everyone has had a person in their lives who has taught them something about their family history and teachings that have been handed down. I learned today that Jane is part Deleware and used to spend time with her grandmother who told stories about living in harmony with nature. |

**Figure 6-5.** Three Ways of Thinking About Text

controlling others or controlling yourself? This has far-reaching consequences and is at the root of many issues that we find in environmental debates today. Reading literary texts like *Spirits* can provide opportunities to introduce students to a more critical reading and discussion of the deeper and more far-reaching issues that are embedded in the story. The topic of critical literacy has been part of an ongoing conversation among literacy educators and critical theorists and researchers. Central to the discussion is the question of how to engage readers in analytical thinking and authentic learning about important political, economic, and social issues, and, at the same time, open up a conversation based on social justice and activism (Powell, Cantrell, Adams, 2001; Luke, 2000; Shor, 1996; Lankshear, McLaren, 1993). I believe that through a critical stance in reading literature, students not only learn to identify and question the explicit and implicit issues that are embedded in a plot, they can also transform their thinking into action that is based on social activism and the desire for positive change.

One way that students can extend the *Thinking* activity into the realm of critical literacy is by searching newspapers, magazines, or other media for stories that deal with some of the environmental debates in play today. Many of the debates, such as the impact of deforestation, the need for wilderness preservation, and the uses of nuclear power, are the same as those that play an integral role in *Spirits*. Learning to connect the underlying issues raised in the text with those affecting their world in this concrete way can open up discussions about ways students can actively participate in these debates and work toward solutions. For example, there are many organizations that provide education and advocate for legislation to protect the environment and those living in negatively impacted areas. Students can become part of these kinds of national and even global efforts through writing congressmen or other world leaders. There may also be local issues that offer opportunities for student involvement, from petitioning to save a neighborhood park to testifying before a school board on curriculum or textbook adoptions. Developing a critical stance in reading can provide students with the ability to ask important questions, as well as help develop an attitude for a democratic citizenry with a purpose toward social justice and the enactment of positive social change.

## Working with Words

One of the most challenging and stimulating aspects of reading *Spirits of the High Mesa* for someone who is not literate in Spanish is the use of Spanish words and sentences interwoven with English throughout the text. If you are not able to read Spanish, you may miss some of the humor that is subtly sprinkled throughout the text. For example, at the beginning of the story, Flavio, in describing radio shows like *The Lone Ranger*, says, "I could never understand why such a smart Indian was called Tonto" (p. 10). You would not get the joke if you did not know that *tonto* means stupid or dumb in Spanish. However, many authors who write primarily English texts that contain some Spanish words or phrases (interlingual writing) also provide clues to help readers who cannot read Spanish so they can construct meaning and gain an understanding of the passage. You may remember, the author of *Silent Dancing* provided such clues.

In addition to single words, there is more inclusion of sentences written in Spanish in *Spirits of the High Mesa*. One device used by the author is to provide an English paraphrase, and sometimes a direct translation, that is stated by one character explaining the Spanish sentence that has been spoken by another character. For example, on page 107, a direct translation is provided. El Grande responds to the question about who killed Luke Evans by saying, *"Todavía no sabemos."* The next sentence provides the meaning: "'We don't know yet,' my father repeated." This technique of providing a direct translation is also used for words, and in some cases the translation is from English to Spanish. For example, on page 78, the word "dangerous" is followed by the Spanish *peligroso.*

Some sentences written in Spanish are explained by giving the reader the general idea rather than a direct translation. For example, on page 110, when Torpe says, *Lo maté por cabrón,"* the explanation is given in the following sentence. "Torpe had just admitted he had killed the gringo in front of everybody." Another way the author provides the English-only reader with meaning for the Spanish text is through context clues given in the surrounding English text. For example, on page 30, El Grande tells Flavio, *"Hijo, siéntate aquí,"* and the sentence is completed in English, "as he pointed to a spot next to the fence." The next sentence provides another clue, as El Grande sits back against the haystack. We gather from El Grande's directive and then his action that both are sitting down for a conversation. Therefore, the reader can make a fairly informed guess from the context that the statement in Spanish is probably one that is telling Flavio to sit by the fence.

Perhaps the most accessible meaning for the English-only reader is provided through the use of *cognates* that the author has carefully chosen to insert in the English text. A comment that is often made by the students who read *Spirits* is, "I don't know any Spanish, but when I read this book, I felt like I could read and understand a lot, even though it was in Spanish." The reason for this is the use of cognates. *Cognate* is a term taken from linguistics that denotes words sharing a similarity of form that is derived from a common parent or root. In other words, a *cognate* is a word that looks the same—spelled the same or nearly the same—in more than one language. The word also denotes the same meaning. There are many words in English that have been "borrowed" from the Spanish and incorporated into the English language. The primary difference between the Spanish word and the English is that they are pronounced somewhat differently. In any case, when an English-only reader encounters the cognate written in the text, the word will be fairly easy to identify and understand. There are different kinds of cognates. The *perfect* cognate is a direct match. For example, *color, popular, natural, terrible,* and *horrible* are spelled the same in Spanish and in English and mean the same thing. In another type of cognate, the *near* match words look very similar in both languages, except for a one- or two-letter difference and maybe an added accent mark or a tilde (~). The reader can still easily identify the words. Many of these words are found in *Spirits*. For example, you can probably read and understand the following words: *emergencia* (p. 24), *importancia* (p. 31), *eléctricos* (p. 32), *renegados* (p. 36), *atómica* (p. 37), *rancho* (p. 83), *disciplina* (p. 132). There are also *false* cognates in which the words appear similar to English words, but their *meanings* are very different. For example, *sopa,* which seems very close to the English word *soap,* is the Spanish word for *soup.* However, the majority of the cognates in *Spirits* are near cognates and thus, easily identifiable and understood.

## Creating a Cognate Lexicon

Students can learn new vocabulary both in Spanish and English by creating a lexicon of cognates. You will need both a Spanish and English dictionary to verify that the cognate is not false. By looking up the word in the *diccionario,* students can also practice their dictionary skills. As you read the story, ask students to identify the words that they think are cognates, write them down, and then look them up in the dictionary. Be sure to include the part of speech and, for Spanish nouns, whether it is masculine or feminine. This designation is usually indicated by either the letter *m* or *f* in parenthesis. This is an important difference in the Spanish language and should be noted. You can also develop a cognate lexicon on a word processor, recording new cognates that are encountered while reading other stories that incorporate Spanish words into English text, and also those that appear in other authentic print sources, such as signs, menus, advertisements, and so forth.

There are also many words in *Spirits* that cannot be found in a standard dictionary because they are popular slang expressions. Some of these words may have a literal meaning or denotation that can be defined; however, the connotation is not directly translatable. For example, the literal translation of *huevos* into English is the word *eggs*. However, if you read the word in context on page 11 of the text, the connotation is something very different.

### Across the Curriculum

As we have mentioned previously, embedded in the story of *Spirits of the High Mesa* are important issues concerning the environment. With the arrival of the *molino* comes logging, which eventually changes the landscape and even affects El Grande's mountain property. We also read about the coming of electrical power, which is generated by the construction of dams, and essentially changes the natural flow of rivers. And, although only briefly mentioned at the beginning of the text, the hint of the destructiveness of nuclear power created in Los Alamos is subtly connected to the high incidence of cancer in humans near nuclear testing, which we read about when Flavio, as an adult, becomes a cancer patient. These national and global issues can be a beginning point for students to conduct inquiries into these issues, which are still at the core of intense debates today.

## The Nuclear Debate

Emphasizing a link between different literary works can strengthen a reader's comprehension of texts. Through intertextual connections, thinking can be extended beyond just one context and can open up different perspectives on the same topic or concept. In Chapter 4 (*Jumping Off to Freedom*), we discussed the historic Cuban Missile Crisis that posed the serious threat of nuclear war between the United States and the Soviet Union. In this chapter, we have discussed the creation of the atomic bomb at the Los Alamos laboratory, which ushered in this new era. This destructive force, however, also offered some benefits as well. Atomic energy is used to generate a portion of the world's electricity, and cancer patients receive radiation therapy for treatment of their illnesses. This two-sided coin of destructiveness and benefits continues to be at the core of great debates about the use of nuclear power. Even on the benefits side there are potential negative effects. For example, the nuclear reactors used to generate power are not without risks. Consider the effects of the accidents involving release of toxic radiation levels at Chernobyl in Ukraine and Tokaimura in Japan.

## Inquiry into the Issues

One way to extend the topic of the development of the atomic bomb that was introduced in the book is to conduct an inquiry into issues surrounding the uses and abuses of nuclear energy. Because the advent of the nuclear age began with the creation of the atomic bomb during World War II, a good place to begin your inquiry is with the historic events carried out at Los Alamos, a place that was just over the mountains from the setting of the novel. Students can approach their inquiry from several different disciplines, depending on their interests. From the historical perspective, students can research the beginnings of the Manhattan Project, in its planning stages at Berkeley, the development of the laboratory at Los Alamos, and finally the testing of the bomb at the Trinity site. From a geographical perspective, students can locate various kinds of maps of the site and surrounding area. From the scientific perspective, students may want to explore the principles of nuclear fission or other aspects of nuclear energy. Students may also want to find biographies of the scientists who played important roles in the project: John Manley, who supervised the early studies that preceded Los Alamos; Joe McKibben, who made the final connections to the test bomb; Edwin McMillan; Ernest Lawrence; Enrico Fermi; and the project's head, J. Robert Oppenheimer.

## Taking a Position and Taking Action

After collecting the information about the discovery and initial use of nuclear energy, students can extend this knowledge into a critical analysis of the different ways nuclear energy is used today. For example, in addition to the manufacturing of nuclear weapons, nuclear energy is also used to generate electricity for homes and businesses. Many governments and governmental agencies, such as the U.S. Environmental Protection Agency (EPA), national and international organizations, and citizens groups, such as Greenpeace and the Sierra Club, have studied and developed informational resources that are either for or against these uses. For example, international organizations such as Greenpeace and Friends of the Earth, advocate against nuclear testing and the development and operation of nuclear power plants. On the other side of the debate are the power companies and governmental agencies that maintain the safety of nuclear power plants and advocate for the benefits, such as electricity, that nuclear power can bring. To get students involved in understanding these issues and beginning to formulate their own positions on these and other important issues, first have students research all the ways nuclear energy is used in the world today. Students can then gather information on the pros and cons of each use. From this information, students should begin to formulate an opinion about how they stand on the issue by incorporating the information gathered. The next step can be either an informal debate of the pros and cons or developing their opinions into a written position paper. I like to use the informal debate as a prewriting activity when working with older students. Many times, using this oral presentation in a debate setting can challenge students to build better arguments for the positions they take in their written papers. A position paper usually consists of the following basic components:

- A statement of the problem or issue that will be presented in the paper
- Identification of important vocabulary and concepts associated with the issue
- A summary of your position on the issue
- Description of the arguments against your position and why they are not valid (in your opinion and in paraphrases or quotations from reliable sources)
- Description of the arguments that support your position (using supporting information and inclusion of quotations from reliable sources)
- A closing statement restating your position and summarizing the validity of your argument

## Extending the Debate

Another issue that was embedded in the story of *Spirits* had to do with the effects of logging on a community that was located in a natural setting. The impact of logging has been a much-debated issue in the United States for a number of years. On both sides of this issue are the U.S. Forest Service and groups such as the Sierra Club. Students can extend their research into the pros and cons of this debate much in the same way as they did on the topic of nuclear energy. Other related environmental debates can also be explored, particularly if you live in an area in which there is a specific concern. For example, there are many urban areas that are involved in ongoing political debates about air quality. There is also an active debate concerning the placement of toxic waste on Native American reservation lands. Students can choose issues that are of interest to them and generate either a paper or flyer that states their position. Creating a flyer can be a good class project to continue the concept of critical literacy introduced earlier in this chapter. To create the flyer, collect the information in the same way you did for the position paper on the nuclear energy debate. To present the information in flyer format, you can gather examples of different kinds of informational flyers. Many of the organizations that you may have accessed for your previous position paper have flyers or similar kinds of informational pages on the Web. Students can then choose the format and create their flyers using the information they have collected about the selected issues. Students should also include a suggestion of how to take action in support of their positions. In this way, they are moving their position statements from the realm of the classroom and into the authentic world.

## Summary

Change is a phenomenon that is a natural part of life. All living things experience change. Even things we consider non-living, such as mountains or volcanoes, go through alterations or changes, which can be brought about by erosion or eruption. Some changes and their effects are brought about by human intervention, in the name of modernization or progress. These changes can be beneficial, and at the same time, they can also have adverse effects. Such a dichotomy is at the core of the conflicts in *Spirits of the High Mesa*. Although it is not possible in many cases to return things to the way they were before the introduction of the changes, as was the case in the story, it is possible to question critically the effects and pose solutions to any problems associated with those changes. The story of *Spirits of the High Mesa* presents an opportunity for a critical literacy approach in which readers can become involved in analytical thinking, authentic learning, and social activism concerning important political, economic, and social issues. But, taking a critical stance does not have to be limited to these larger systems' issues or implemented in the context of a school-based literacy activity. As human beings, we continually face making personal choices that can effect change in our lives. Sometimes the choices we make bring about changes that are beneficial for us as well as for those who share our world. At other times, choices reflect a dilemma that can have both good and bad effects. Still other choices can bring changes that have dangerous consequences for everyone involved, even those outside of our personal, inner circle. Regardless of the scope or context of the issues involved, or whether they are in the public or private sphere, at the heart of the matter is the ability to question critically all sides of the problem in order to make an informed choice that leads to positive action. Without this ability, we become disempowered, passive objects *of* change rather than active agents *for* change.

# Chapter 7

# ...y no se lo tragó la tierra/
# And the Earth Did Not Devour Him:
# The Voices of the People

## Story Summary

The diverse narrative structure of Rivera's classic work gives the reader a unique glimpse into the art and craft of the oral storyteller who carries the different voices of the people in memory and relates their histories in order to preserve their culture. Using the stylistic element of different points of view, the author tells his stories as an omniscient third-person narrator, in the child's voice of a first-person narrator, through dialogue between the many voices of the Chicano collective, and through dramatic monologues that reflect innermost thoughts. Using personal experiences, observations of others' experiences, and fragments of conversations about daily life in the fields, in the home, and at school, the boy narrator attempts to reconstruct his own memory of a figurative year that was lost to him (p. 7/83).

In the previous chapter on *Spirits of the High Mesa,* we discussed a number of ways that authors develop characters in a story. In ...*y no se lo tragó la tierra/And the earth did not devour him,* characterization is taken to its highest level. The stories are presented to the reader through short vignettes and longer episodes that incorporate descriptive narrative, dialogue, and dramatic monologue. Through these three forms, Rivera presents a holistic picture of the culture of the migrant farm worker. The book opens with descriptive narrative, related by the third-person narrator. In this introduction, the reader learns of the narrator's desire to reconstruct a year of his life—perhaps his whole history and identity—that was lost in his memory. This opening narrative serves to frame the sketches that follow and seem to be a metaphor for the art and craft of the storyteller whose calling is to reconstruct and keep the memory of a collective cultural consciousness. The same structure of descriptive narrative is found throughout the book. For example, in the episode in which the character is denied service at the barbershop and access to the movie theatre, we discover, along with the subject of the sketch, the racism and discrimination against the young boy who represents the collective farm worker identity. There are also family-related memories, such as the short sketch of a grandfather and his youthful and impatient grandson, as well as the story of a beautiful wedding day. There are memories of school, such as the one about the child's sacrifice of a button for a school poster. Through the voice of this third-person narrator, the reader also experiences the dramatic irony and skepticism that underscores the various stories. We hear stories lived in the familiarity of family and those shared collectively with the community of farm workers. We also hear those about a life lived in the often alien and harsh environments of school and society.

Descriptive narrative is also used to introduce the dramatic structure of dialogue that is played out in social situations using the language associated with the actors in a specific social context. In this blending of structures, narrative is woven in and out of the dialogue, mixing the voice of the third-person narrator with the voices of the unidentified people who speak to one another. For example, in "Los niños no se aguantaron"/"The children couldn't wait," the stage is set for the tragic event of the shooting of a child who stops working to get a drink of water. We learn from this introductory narrative that when the heat had set in early, the bucket of drinking water the boss had brought into the fields was not enough to relieve everyone's thirst, especially the children.

When the children begin to go to the water tank at the edge of the field, the boss gets angry because the loss of time picking means he must pay more since it is an hourly wage. We then hear the voices of the field worker and his child and whether they should risk going for a drink at the tank. This dialogue is followed by a narrative passage describing the shooting incident. The episode ends with a dialogue between the farm workers discussing the demise of the boss, who reaps the harvest of his own injustice, ending up in poverty and a state of drunken, guilt-ridden madness, driven to suicide. However, the underlying question of justice not being satisfied according to the law (isn't murder punishable by death?) seems to come through the stated question, "But he didn't kill himself, did he?" In other words, in the end, the crime of murder was neither acknowledged nor punished by the recognized laws of society.

There are other similar episodes related through dialogue with an intermingling of third-person narrative. One of the longer episodes in particular, "La noche que se apagaron las luces"/"The night of the blackout," tells of a love triangle that reaches a violent climax at a dance, a well-known and often repeated theme in oral as well as written Mexican-American and Chicano literature (Kanellos, 1986). In this written version of this traditional tragic tale, the story of Ramon and Juanita is related through the narrator as well as through dialogue between the ill-fated lovers and those who know them.

Dialogue is also used in the shorter sketches and is similar both in content and language to the *actos* in Chicano theatre. In these short, dramatic acts, archetypal characters present typical scenes from Chicano life filled with tragedy, humor, and social satire (Kanellos, 1986). The plight of the itinerant worker who is at the mercy of often unscrupulous bosses is humorously and yet satirically portrayed in the scene in which two *compadres* are discussing the location and even existence of a place called Utah.

Sometimes the narrative form shifts to first person, as in "La mano en la bolsa"/"Hand in his pocket." In this episode, the first-person narrator describes his experience living with Don Laito and Doña Bone. Inserted in the narrative are bits of dialogue spoken by these two characters. First-person narrative is also used with longer dialogic sections as in "El retrato"/"The Portrait" that tells the story of a fraudulent portrait salesman.

Finally, some of the stories also incorporate the use of dramatic monologue or an inner dialogue of thought. For example, in "Es que duele"/"It's that it hurts," the narrator is speaking through a monologue that exposes his inner thoughts about the humiliation he must go through at school and the shame he feels when he fears he has been expelled from school. The irony of the story unfolds as the child expresses his confusion about whether he has actually been expelled: "But, maybe they didn't expel me, *sure they did*, maybe not, *sure they did*" (p. 95). This confusion is just one very real example of the difficulties that children must face when the language of school is not their first language. Other characters also reveal their innermost thoughts through these dramatic monologues. For example, in "Un rezo"/"The prayer," a mother pours out her heart and soul for her son's safe return from the Korean War. The use of monologue is also mixed with the other forms of dialogue and descriptive narrative. For example, in "La noche buena"/"The night before Christmas," Doña María determines to venture out into the city to buy her children toys for Christmas. Her dramatic monologue expresses her anxiety about the journey into a hostile environment where store clerks view her suspiciously. The use of dialogue at the end of the piece reveals the underlying reason for her anxiety—a prejudice reflecting a predetermined stereotypical notion of migrant worker as thief.

Thus, it is in ...*y no se lo tragó la tierra*, that author-storyteller Rivera reconstructs the memory of the collective migrant worker experience. His characterizations shift from a third-person to a first-person narrator who tells the stories about the events and archetypal characters with a keen observer's eye, to the dialogues (of overheard conversations) between family members and between farm workers, to the monologues that reveal the character's innermost thoughts. Rivera accomplishes this reconstruction of a collective memory through his use of these written structural forms that are based on oral language, which is historically the medium of storyteller.

## Building Background Before You Read

When was the last time you visited the supermarket or corner store to buy some fruit and vegetables? When you were choosing a head of lettuce or squeezing the peaches or thumping the melon, did you ever think about how all of this produce ended up at the market, ready for you to buy when you wanted it? The complex cycle of agricultural production is essentially invisible to the average consumer, yet, at the heart of this cycle, is the little known, but indispensable, migrant farm worker. While the migrant population is somewhat diverse, it is estimated that the majority of workers are mostly Hispanics/Latinos—Mexican Americans, Mexican Nationals, Puerto Ricans, Cubans, and citizens of Central and South America. Many of these workers live apart from their families, in work camps for single men. However, many of these workers, particularly those who follow the Midwestern picking routes, travel with their families to these sites. This labor force has been working in the fields for many years and generations. In the novel, ...*y no se lo tragó la tierra/And the earth did not devour him,* Tomás Rivera tells the story of the people who are part of this community.

## The Migrant Farm Worker

The story of the Mexican-American migrant farm worker is part of a complex set of economic and ecological forces that began in the mid-nineteenth century, soon after the Emancipation Proclamation and the end of the U.S. Civil War. The end of legalized slavery in the United States brought about a shortage in farm labor because many former slaves were no longer working the fields. This created a demand for low-cost farm workers. In the Southwest, many Mexican Americans, who had become citizens of the United States after the signing of the Treaty of Guadalupe Hidalgo with Mexico, filled these low-wage jobs, which also meant extremely poor working and living conditions. Beginning in the early twentieth century, many Mexican nationals were recruited to meet the demand for farm labor in the rapidly growing Southwest. The Immigration Act of 1924 put a moratorium on immigrant groups other than Mexican workers. Border stations were set up to admit these immigrants, and a head tax was assessed for each person who legally entered the United States from Mexico on a permanent visa. There were no quotas for this wave of Mexican immigration. In addition to the legal immigrants, many Mexican nationals entered the United States illegally to avoid the border immigration fees, which were costly. Shortly after World War I, an economic recession led to a drop in the market price of farm crops. This brought about farmers' attempts to increase their productivity in order to gain back the money lost. This push to produce more crops also meant cultivation of more land using more mechanized farm equipment, all of which required more money, causing many farmers to overextend their budgets. When the stock market crashed in 1929, the already overextended farmers lost their land, and the tenant farmers working for the larger landowners found themselves unable to find work.

In addition to this economic disaster, there were also disastrous environmental consequences that came with the increased cultivation of land, which had replaced the natural grasslands of the southern Great Plains of the United States. As a result, the rich soil lost its ability to retain water that the grasslands had conserved, the nutrients slowly washed away, and the land began to erode. When a seventeen-year drought began in 1931, followed by the beginning of the severe dust storms, resulting from the eroding land, many of the farms literally dried up and blew away. The area became known as the Dust Bowl. The onslaught of the Great Depression, coupled with drought and the accompanying dust storms, forced thousands of farmers and their families to join the stream of migrant farm work.

## The Bracero Program

The World War II era was a time of labor shortage in the United States. In August of 1942, the United States and Mexico entered into an agreement, creating the Bracero Program. This program contributed significantly to the growth of the agricultural economy for the United States. More than three million Mexican farm laborers came to work the fields as part of this program. The braceros cultivated the agricultural fields of our country into the most productive in the world. Experienced farm workers, the braceros came from the principal agricultural regions of Mexico. Convinced they would earn a great deal of money, the braceros left their homes and families to work the fields on the other side of the border. However, the reality for the bracero meant low wages and a poverty-level existence. The braceros also suffered from prejudicial treatment, harassment, and oppression from racist extremist groups and even government authorities. By the 1960s, however, an excess of agricultural workers, both legal and illegal, and new farming technology supplanted the practicality and need for the Bracero Program. Thus, the Bracero Program, which has been described as a system of legalized slavery, officially ended in 1964. However, braceros continue to cross the borders into the Southwestern United States to work in the fields and on ranches. They also continue to be one of the most exploited and oppressed labor groups in the United States.

## César Chávez and the United Farm Workers Union

The most influential person in the history of the Mexican-American farm worker movement was César Chávez. During the 1960s and 1970s, Chávez became a household name as he actively promoted and worked for *La Causa*, the cause of the migrant worker. Born near Yuma, Arizona, in 1927, Chávez learned early about injustice. Losing their land through a broken agreement and foreclosure as a result of dishonest dealings, the Chávez family moved to California. César Chávez's experience with school was not a pleasant one. The teachers were mostly Anglo and the students could only speak English at school, a rule that was enforced by corporal punishment in the form of a rap on the knuckles with a ruler. In school, Chávez had to endure racist remarks and experience the signs of institutional racism that read *For Whites Only*. Despite this oppressive environment, similar to that described in Rivera's novel, Chávez graduated from eighth grade in 1942 and then went to work in the fields. In 1944 he joined the navy and served for two years. After he returned to San Jose, he met Fred Ross, a community organizer. Working for Ross's organization, the Community Service Organization (CSO), Chávez's job was to get people registered to vote. From then on, he became a committed grass-roots activist.

While working with the CSO, Chávez met Dolores Huerta, who also worked for the CSO. During this time, they came to the conclusion that farm workers needed to be organized into unions. In 1962, Chávez and Dolores Huerta founded the National Farm Workers Association (NFW), which later became the United Farm Workers Union (UFW). Through the NFW and later the UFW, Chávez and Huerta lobbied the government for economic aid to unemployed and underemployed farm workers, and organized nonviolent marches, boycotts, pickets, and strikes to improve conditions and pay for them. One of the most famous of such marches was the 340-mile trek from Delano to Sacramento, California, in 1966. This march brought attention to the Delano grape strike so that people would become aware of the need for better pay and safer working conditions for those who worked in the fields.

Chávez, who was willing to sacrifice his own life to forward *La Causa*, fasted in nonviolent protest on a number of occasions. In 1968, he fasted for 25 days, drinking only water. He fasted again in 1972 for 24 days. In 1988, his fast lasted for 36 days. Through fasting, Chávez wanted to demonstrate his belief that only through nonviolent sacrifice and hard work could the union survive and enact positive change. Fasting for Chávez was a personal act of purification and cleansing as well as for those who worked with him in the farm worker movement; it was also an act to place moral pressure on those who were in positions of authority to enact social and labor-relations changes. Chávez died in 1993, near Yuma, Arizona; his greatly weakened heart finally gave out from all of the fasting. On August 8, 1994, Helen Chávez, César's widow, accepted the Medal of Freedom for her late husband, and it was presented by President Bill Clinton.

There are numerous books about the life and work of César Chávez. The UFW website also is a good resource for his speeches. Two notable recent titles about Chávez are *The Fight in the Fields: César Chávez and the Farm Workers Movement* and *The Rhetorical Career of César Chávez*.

## Tomás Rivera

Tomás Rivera was born in Crystal City, Texas, in 1935. A child of migrant farm workers, Rivera and his family followed the migrant stream from Texas to various other states where they worked in the fields, often under oppressive and harsh working and living conditions. Rivera was an avid reader and began writing at an early age. Through his determination and overcoming great obstacles, he graduated from high school and earned a bachelor's degree from college, the first of his family to do so. A teacher, he taught for many years in Texas public schools in San Antonio, Crystal City, and League City. After receiving his doctorate in Romance Languages and Literature from the University of Oklahoma in 1971, Rivera became a professor of Spanish at the University of Texas at San Antonio, and in 1973, he was appointed an associate dean and vice-president of the university in 1976. In 1978, Rivera left San Antonio to become executive vice-president of the University of Texas at El Paso. Then in 1979, Tomás Rivera became the first Mexican-American chancellor in the United States, at the University of California, Riverside. In addition to his own career in teaching and writing, Rivera was dedicated to helping Mexican Americans gain access to higher education as well as opening doors to the writing and publishing world.

Rivera wrote various literary works, including poetry, but probably his most famous work is the novel, …*y no se lo tragó la tierra/And the earth did not devour him,* which was published in 1970. For this work, Rivera received the Quinto Sol Literary Award in 1971. The novel was originally written in Spanish and later translated into English. The original Spanish text is written in the colloquial speech of the working-class migrant worker and, as such, is highly expressive of an orality that is at the root of the storytelling tradition. For the reader of Spanish, this oral rhythm is evident. For the English-only reader, the oral rhythm is an approximation. For this reason, if possible, it would be good to read the Spanish text aloud (followed by the English translation), so that English-only speakers and readers can hear and appreciate the oral rhythm of the work.

…*y no se lo tragó la tierra/And the earth did not devour him* is a landmark in Mexican-American literature, both a documentary and a literary work of art. As an author, Rivera said he was influenced by his readings of James Joyce, William Faulkner, and the great Latin American novelists. Rivera also credited Mexican American anthropologist and folklorist Americo Paredes as being a great influence. Many scholars and friends believe this work to be autobiographical, documenting his experiences and the overheard conversations from the community of migrant workers of which he was a part. Through the different voices making up the social and historical context of the farm worker in the late 1940s and 1950s in Texas, Rivera presents a holistic portrait of the lifestyle, culture, and worldview of the Mexican-American migrant worker. For a more in-depth study of Rivera and his work, Julián Olivares, *International Studies in Honor of Tomás Rivera,* is an excellent resource. The various chapters offer recollections and essays about the novel as well as different aspects of his work in relation to other Chicano literature.

## Reading and Responding to the Story

In the novel *y no se lo tragó la tierra/…And the earth did not devour him,* Rivera uses the written forms of dialogue and monologue as well as descriptive narrative. Through these forms, the reader is given concrete examples of the stylistic element of *point of view*. The dialogues that are spoken in the voices of the people of the fields, the monologues that represent the interior language of a person's thought, and the narrative of an omniscient third-person or first-person observer share a sense of orality that is at the root of the Hispanic storytelling tradition. Through these voices, the reader learns about the migrant worker experience and culture. Within these stories we hear a collective voice that often speaks with irony that, through its understated subtlety, illuminates the message of discrimination and social injustice. Because of the richness of style and content, the activities described in this chapter focus on helping students develop their understanding of the literary elements used in the novel, as well as responding to the content of the text.

## Examining the Forms

The opening episode of the novel is a descriptive narrative related through a third-person narrator. The narrator seems to know about the person being described in terms of observable events as well as interior motives and thoughts. The following episode is also told in third person. As you progress through the novel, the reader encounters other forms—first-person descriptive narrative, dialogue, and monologue—in various combinations. As students read the novel, they can identify the different forms and shifts of point of view within a given episode. The example below illustrates one kind of graphic organizer that can be used to identify the different narrative forms and points of view found in the novel. See Figure 7-1.

## Isn't It Ironic?

A few years ago, a teacher and I were having a conversation about how hard it is for students to identify the use of irony in literary works, not to mention asking them to interpret it. At that time, there was a popular tune by Alanis Morissette that consisted of a set of vignettes followed by the question "Isn't it ironic?"

| Episode Title or First Line | 1st person Narrative | 3rd person Narrative | Dialogue | Monologue |
|---|---|---|---|---|
| "Lo que nunca supo"/"What his mother never knew" (9/85) | | X | | |
| "Los niños no se aguantaron"/ "The children couldn't wait" (10/86) | | X | X | |
| "Un rezo"/ "A prayer" (14/90) | | | | X |
| "Es que duele"/"It's that it hurts" (16/92) | | | X | X |
| "El retrato"/ "The portrait" (60/136) | X | | X | |

**Figure 7-1.** Forms and Points of View

Thinking of using a piece of popular culture to teach irony to her English class, she designed a lesson using the song as an example. The teacher said that while her students really liked and related to the tune, they still didn't get the concept of irony or the meaning intended by the songwriter.

So, why is irony such a difficult concept to grasp for many students? One reason may be related to a similar difficulty in vocabulary acquisition and reading comprehension that occurs when trying to move from a surface level of understanding to a deeper meaning or interpretation. Since *irony* is based on an incongruity or a discrepancy between what is stated and what is really meant, the connection between surface and deep meaning seems to fit. If we can manage to help students understand irony, we may be able to connect this concept to their understanding of surface and deep meaning of words and text.

The word *irony* comes from the Greek *eiron*, a comic character in Greek drama who typically spoke in seemingly simple words that hid deep and complex meanings. There are three kinds of irony used in literary works:

- *Dramatic irony* occurs when an audience/reader perceives something that a character does not know, giving the audience a sense of being in on something that the character is unaware of. It may also occur between characters, when one or more individual characters know something another character does not know.

- *Verbal irony* occurs when a character says one thing, but really means something else.
- *Situational irony* occurs when there is an incongruity between what is expected to happen and the actual results of the situation.

In this chapter, we will focus on verbal and situational irony. A good example of the use of irony in the novel can be found in *Los quemaditos/Little burnt victims*. In this tragic story of children's death in a house fire in which the only things left on the victims are the boxing gloves that their father had given them, the dialogue at the end of the story points to this ironic paradox. When the question is raised, "But I wonder why the gloves didn't burn," the answer is that, ". . . these people know how to make things so well that not even fire will touch them" (pp. 121–122). The verbal irony, is that "these people" exercise great care in making indestructible the materialistic things they consider valuable, but have little invested in protecting a "commodity" such as a migrant worker child (Kanellos, 1986). The situational irony is that the gloves would be untouched by the fire.

To develop students' understanding of irony, you might begin with situational irony because evidence of it can be identified in more concrete terms. In other words, we can better see the relationship between our expectations about how something might turn out, and the sometimes very different results. Ask students to brainstorm some situations taken from their personal experiences in which they were expecting one thing to happen, but something totally unexpected happened instead. I like to use large pieces of craft paper tacked up all around the room—a kind of graffiti wall. Make two columns on each sheet and label them *Expectations* (How they thought it would turn out) and *Happening* (How it actually turned out). After the students have spent time at the graffiti wall, discuss students' written responses and if and how they are examples of situational irony. Then, as students read the novel, ask them to try to find examples of situational irony in the text.

The move to verbal irony can be made through its relationship to sarcasm. Students are well familiar with sarcasm. How many times have you heard sarcastic statements like "Really nice hairdo," or "Good-looking shoes," when the real meaning was just the opposite. Ask students to think about statements in which they knew that the meaning was very different from what was said. Then, as you read the story of *Los quemaditos/Little burnt victims,* discuss the dialogue in which irony is used. Ask students to write a journal entry that gives their interpretation of the statement about the boxing gloves being the only things that survived the fire and why that might be considered irony.

## Teatro Chicano

The use of dialogue in the novel is highly dramatic in recreating events in an authentic way, such that the reader is actually experiencing the situations along with the characters engaged in conversation. Many of the episodes in the novel are almost entirely presented in dialogue. These dialogues are very similar to Chicano theatre skits, which have a long-standing tradition in Mexican folkdrama (Kanellos, 1986). According to Kanellos (1986), the most recent manifestation of this tradition is *teatro chicano* (Chicano theatre). In this traveling theatre, improvisational skits or *actos* present scenes from the barrio or the fields through authentic dialogue in Spanish, English, and combinations of both, depending on the situation being presented. In Chapter 5 (*Trino's Choice*), we also talked about El Teatro Campesino, a dramatic improvisational troupe founded as part of the United Farm Workers Union by Luis Valdez, and the important role that it played in the development of contemporary Mexican-American and Chicano literature. Some of the episodes in *...y no se lo tragó la tierra* are very similar in content, language, and format to the *actos* of *teatro chicano.*

An authentic way for students to respond to the text is through performance of these dialogues like the *actos* of *teatro chicano.* If there are Spanish speakers in the class, the *actos* can first be performed in Spanish, and then a translation performance can be done using the English text. In actual *teatro chicano* performances, the skit is introduced by one of the troupe members. Since some of the dialogues in the novel have a preceding narrative, this can be read, or students may want to write and present their own introductions. Another production technique that is part of *teatro chicano* is the use of signs that explain the relationship of the characters to one another. For example, characters may wear signs such as *La Mamá/Mother, El Patroncito/Boss, El Hijo/Son,* and so on. Presentation in this authentic way can reinforce comprehension of the novel and provide an opportunity for responding to the text through creative expression. Using dramatic interpretation as a response to the novel moves the words off the page and into the realm of orality that is at the core of both the theatre and storytelling traditions.

## Responding through Interior Monologue

As stated earlier, another narrative form that is used effectively in the novel is *the interior monologue.* In an interior monologue, the actor or character presents a personal reflection, an introspective view, of his or her innermost thoughts. When reading or listening to an interior monologue, the audience gains insight into what the character is really thinking or feeling about the situations of life he or she is experiencing. It is like a little window into the soul of the person who is speaking. Some definitions of interior monologue link the technique to *stream of consciousness* in which the character's flow of thought is revealed in sensory images and free associations. However, many literary theorists consider the technique of interior monologue as more structured in its presentation of rational thoughts, closely related to *soliloquy* and *dramatic monologue.*

To get inside a person's or character's head is a difficult thing, because we cannot, after all, really know everything a person may be thinking, even if he tells us. More importantly, our individual cultural and experiential backgrounds frame our assumptions and interpretations to the extent that it is probably impossible to actually think like someone else. However, considering what others may be thinking or feeling is important in building empathy and twofold understanding: first, that cultural perspectives other than one's own exist; and, second, that while they may be different from one's own perspective, these must be respected and treated with dignity.

After students read the novel, ask them to pick one of the characters in one of the episodes and write an interior monologue for that character. It is important to remember to use language that is in the expressive mode of speaking rather than narrating or telling; it must also convey an introspective and reflective examination of the character's innermost thoughts and motivations. A good brainstorming activity to use for a prewrite is to ask students to create a list of questions that they would like to ask the character. For example, the character of Ramon in *La noche que se apagaron las luces/The night the lights went out,* provokes many questions:

- How did you feel when you saw Juanita dancing with someone else?
- Why did you love someone who did not love you in the same way?
- What were you thinking when you stormed out of the dance hall?
- What made you walk over to the power plant?
- If you had it to do all over again, would you change anything?

Then, by answering these questions as if they were the character, students have ideas to begin a draft of their interior monologues. Once revised and completed, the monologues should be performed orally. If students are literate in Spanish, they can write and perform their monologues in Spanish with an English translation.

### Working with Words

When we think about the term narrative, essentially we think of telling stories about people involved in events that take place in a particular place and time. Descriptive narrative is, therefore, a story, an episode, a vignette that is developed using sensory details designed to bring the reader into the scene as an active participant. These narratives can be written in the point of view of either first or third person. Descriptive narratives can stand alone, be used as an opening paragraph to grab the reader's attention, and can be interwoven with sections of dialogue, all of which we have encountered in Rivera's novel.

The use of sensory details is important to descriptive narrative. The use of carefully chosen descriptors can create an image so real that often we find ourselves in the space and time of the story, hearing the characters speak, feeling the heat or the cold, and experiencing the sights, sounds, smells of the moment. So, how do writers know which words to choose? How do we help our students go about selecting descriptive words that best convey the image without sounding like they swallowed a thesaurus? First, they must really understand the meaning of a word, make it their own. Only then can they have the freedom to knead it and shape it into its expressive form. Therefore, learning new words and acquiring vocabulary requires an understanding of both a word's *denotative* and *connotative* meanings.

## Denotation and Connotation

Words have two kinds of meaning that are termed denotation and connotation. When we refer to a word's denotation, we are talking about the literal meaning or its definition. When we look up a word in a dictionary, we are accessing its denotation. There can be several such denotations and each can involve explanations of different parts of speech that may denote different meanings. For example, the word *book* can be a noun, in which case it denotes a printed text, and it can also be a verb—we can *book* a ticket, or police *book* a prisoner. When we teach dictionary skills, then, we are helping students to access a word's denotation. But, there is another meaning that is a suggested meaning beyond the literal meaning. A word's connotation carries with it values and judgments, as well as historical and cultural associations that have been handed down or evolved from one generation to the next. It could also be argued that certain words have more status than others, and attaining a certain vocabulary can be considered a thing of worth (Bourdieu, 1986).

Some words may have the same denotation but have very different connotations. For example, think of the following pairs of words: house/home, unmarried woman/spinster, angry/enraged, cheap/inexpensive, quiz/test. Now think about how you reacted to each of the words in the pair. Did one evoke a more positive image? Many times our reactions to different connotations reflect our personal experiences with the concept that the word represents. For example, the word *wake,* in which the denotative meaning is a gathering of mourners for one who has died, may connote a very sad and disturbing event for many people. However, in my family, a wake was a joyous time in which the family—aunts, uncles, cousins, grandparents, great-aunts, great-uncles, and so on, got together to visit with each other and tell stories and relive old memories. So, for me, the connotation of the word *wake* evokes a positive response.

So what does this mean for descriptive narrative? If a writer or storyteller is trying to create an image in the mind of the audience, he or she needs to know both the denotative and connotative meanings and anticipate how the audience might respond—positively, negatively, or even neutrally. Rivera creates images that are built on the interplay between denotative and connotative meanings of the words he uses to describe the events and characters in the novel's episodes. For example, in *Los ninos no se aguantaron/The children couldn't wait,* the boss wanted to teach the field worker and his child a lesson—not to take time out of work to get a drink from the water tank. The notion of teaching someone a lesson can have a variety of denotative and connotative meanings. When I think of the concept of teaching, the principal denotation for me involves developing students' knowledge through instruction or example. This meaning connotes a reciprocal relationship in which both teacher and student are involved in a collaborative construction of meaning. However, for others, teaching someone a lesson may have another connotation, such as a punishment or one associated with disciplinary measures. For me, the first connotation evokes a positive response. On the other hand, the example associated with punishment stimulates a negative response. In the text example, the idea that using a gun to teach someone a lesson, regardless of whether the intention was to harm or not, is a connotation that evokes a negative response for me as reader of the story. Can you find other examples in the text in which Rivera portrays an image through the interplay of denotative and connotative meanings? To build understanding of denotation and connotation and connect these meanings to students' experiences, have them compile a word bank of meanings associated with the text. Students should begin by selecting a scene or character from the story that has stimulated a significant personal response or connection. Next, record the primary meaning that the particular words or images denote. Then record what that meaning connotes in the text. Finally, compare the textual connotation with the connotation you usually associate with the words or images. For both connotative meanings, use a plus (+) sign, minus (−) sign, or a 0 (zero) to show whether they evoke positive, negative, or neutral feelings. Using the previous example of "teaching a lesson," a graphic representation might look like this. See Figure 7-2.

Developing an understanding of the concepts of denotation and connotation through the use of textual examples and links to one's own personal experience can help students better grasp the connections and interplay between explicit and implicit mean-

| Image | Denotation | Textual Connotation | Personal Connotation |
|-------|------------|---------------------|----------------------|
| Teaching someone a lesson | Instructing or modeling a skill or strategy | Inflicting fear or harm to change someone's behavior (–) | Reciprocal relationship based in collaborative construction of meaning (+) |

**Figure 7-2.** Denotative and Connotative Meanings

ings of words and descriptive phrases, which promotes greater comprehension of text.

## Across the Curriculum

Although it is primarily a story of an Anglo family's experience during the Great Depression, the publication of John Steinbeck's *Grapes of Wrath* in 1939 first brought the conditions and plight of migrant workers to the forefront for mainstream Americans. However, other sources, such as documentary photography, also provide a different perspective on the stories of the migrant workers, including Mexican and Mexican-American farm workers during the Great Depression.

## Documentary Photography

One of the programs of Franklin D. Roosevelt's New Deal program created during the Great Depression was the Farm Security Administration (FSA). You may remember that the Rural Electrification Association (REA) discussed in Chapter 6 (*Spirits of the High Mesa*) was also part of this multifaceted program. The FSA, which grew out of the Resettlement Administration and moved to the Department of Agriculture in 1937, was created to provide assistance to the rural poor and agricultural migrant workers. The FSA included a plan for documentation of the program through photography. A group of about twenty men and women worked under Roy E. Stryker to create a pictorial record of the effects of the Depression on rural farm workers. After more than sixty years and three generations of their creation, these photographs still remain as striking documents from which Americans can gain a visual understanding of the Great Depression. Perhaps one of the most famous of the photographs is Dorothea Lange's 1936 portrait entitled *Migrant Mother.* Other photographers who participated in this project were Walker Evans, Ben Shahn, Marion Post Wolcott, and Arthur Rothstein.

To begin the study of this era of documentary photography, ask students to gather reproductions of the photographs produced as part of the FSA. These can be found in traditional texts about the Great Depression, and, there are also reproductions on many Internet sites. After viewing these images, ask students to record their initial responses to the individual images. How did the photograph make you feel? Did the photograph remind you of something else?

Now consider the photograph through a more critical "lens." A photograph has often been referred to as a reflection of reality. We have all heard the saying "Cameras don't lie." However, like any other text, a photographic image is an interpretation of reality, a version of what is really there. When photographers take photographs, they focus in on the image they wish to portray, including certain aspects of their subjects, leaving out others. Even after the negative is developed, cropping of the image can further manipulate the "reality." Ask students to respond critically to the photographs as documentary texts. These questions might help start the discussion.

- Why did the photographer choose the particular subject?
- What is the composition of the photograph—the specific subjects, the landscape, and the objects?
- What are some things that could have been added to the image? What could have been left out?
- How does the arrangement of the composition contribute to the overall effect?

Documentary photography is still used to record the social,

economic, and political circumstances that continue to affect migrant farm workers. Students can collect documentary photographic images from over the past decades to the present and compare them for their content and their effect. A chronological presentation of all the photographs should include a discussion of whether there are similarities in the images and what, if any, changes have occurred over the years of documentation. In order to make further connections to the text, ask students to reread the episode *El retrato/The Portrait*. Then, using what they have learned from these photographic images, ask students to write a response to the story.

## You Do the Math

What if you had a family of four and had to feed, house, and clothe them on an income of between $5,000 and $7,500 per year? It seems an impossible task. Yet, many migrant farm worker families are faced with such a dilemma. In addition, most do not have health insurance to cover the many illnesses that are related to the hazards of the job and living in poverty: parasitic infections, tuberculosis, heat stress, toxic chemical injuries, malnutrition, and dental disease, to name a few. Constructing a budget that includes allocations for housing, food, and clothing can provide students with a concrete example of the reality that many migrant families face. Students can break into inquiry teams to study the average costs of groceries, rent, utilities, transportation, and clothing. A trip to the supermarket as well as to other department stores as comparative shoppers can provide students with good examples of prices for food and clothing. Classified ads can be resources for determining rental costs. Utilities companies and public transportation systems can be contacted for rates. After these are collected, students can then construct a budget for the year, choosing what to purchase and for how much. A good way to calculate spending is to break out the costs per month, beginning with a maximum amount available for each month and then listing the expenses. For example, if a family makes $7,500 in a year, the monthly spending cap is $625. The budget can be represented on a spreadsheet, a chart, or other graphic organizer.

## Health Risks and Hazardous Pesticides

Farm workers suffer the highest rate of toxic chemical injuries in the United States, according to the Farm Worker Health Alliance. Cesar Chávez addressed this issue in many of his speeches. The use of pesticides in the fields poses threats of birth defects and cancer in children and adults. Campaigns have been conducted to ban such pesticides. Some have been successful, such as the one that eventually led to the banning of DDT. However, many toxic pesticides remain in use. Students can conduct an inquiry into the types of pesticides used on various crops and the risks attached to each. Using the writing components of a position paper, which were discussed in Chapter 6 (*Spirits of the High Mesa*), students can write a position paper about the use of toxic pesticides in the fields. Students can also become involved with advocacy groups that provide education and seek legislation banning such carcinogens. In addition to the UFW, other private agencies provide ways for citizens to advocate for the protection of farm workers and their families against these harmful pesticides.

## Summary

Tomás Rivera's ...*y no se lo tragó la tierra/And the earth did not devour him* is a landmark piece of Chicano literature that presents a sensitive, true-to-life portrayal of the Chicano farm worker experience. The book, which is a collection of vignettes and episodes taken from the fields and barrios, can be read on many different levels and from a variety of perspectives. As a documentary work, Rivera presents an insider's view of a community that shares a common history and culture, which is similar to the participant observer conducting and writing about an ethnographic study. On another level, Rivera's word portraits, drawn in descriptive narrative, dialogue, and monologue, are as vivid and alive as the photographs of the documentary photojournalist. And, many of the short vignettes and longer episodes reflect the format of Chicano theatre, which is a dramatic presentation of social reality (Kanellos, 1986). The text also naturally lends itself to reading and visualizing these moments in Chicano history and culture through a criticalist lens (Kincheloe, McLaren, 1994; Carspecken, 1996), from which social inequalities and injustices are revealed, and action is taken to change the status quo. Finally, this classic work is often approached and read as a high form of literature. Through the forms of descriptive narrative, dialogue, and monologue, the narrative point of view shifts back and forth, moving the reader to different vantage points that allow glimpses into the lives of the Chicano people whose voices are heard through the text. Like poetry, the *voices* should be read aloud. If possible, it should be read in the Spanish version, which reflects the rich orality and vocabulary of Chicano speech. In doing so, the reader/listener can experience the history, culture, and collective identity, which are held in memory and told in the voices of the Chicano farm workers who worked the fields of Midwest United States and lived in the barrios of Texas.

# Chapter 8

## The Story Continues

At the outset of this book, I stated that this text was about different ways that teachers can help students negotiate the process of reading and construct meanings from texts. The key ingredient in this process is the connection that readers make with the text. When readers approach texts, they bring with them their prior knowledge and lived experiences. In this transaction between reader and text, which has been described by Rosenblatt (1978) and others, the knowledge and experience of the reader come together with the knowledge and experience presented in the text, resulting in an ongoing construction of meanings. In this transaction process, it is important for the reader to be able to find some connections with his or her experiential background and knowledge base. Culturally relevant texts provide pathways to meaning because they can establish strong connections to students' prior knowledge and life experiences. Using this tenet as a guiding principle, I have suggested strategies that can help students construct meanings through the cultural resources represented by the various young adult novels, because I believe that the cultural connections established between text and reader are important for comprehension. However, in addition to thinking of comprehension in terms of a single text, or an *intra*textual reading, we also need to consider the importance of making connections between various texts, which is referred to as intertextuality (Hartman, 1994).

### Connections between Texts

In a study conducted with students reading multiple passages,

Hartman (1994) found that these readers' understandings of one passage connected and contributed to their understandings of prior and future passages. This suggests that meanings are continually being constructed and reconstructed as relationships within and between different texts are established. Thus, given the importance of making connections between different texts to the process of comprehending, we, as teachers, need to provide opportunities for students to read a variety of texts that will foster their ability to read intertextually.

There are several threads that connect the different young adult novels represented in this book, which can provide opportunities for intertextual reading. Perhaps the strongest thread, woven through all of the texts, is represented by the theme of identity. In each text, a relationship and dialogue with the physical, psychological, and socio-cultural factors that contribute to the continual creation and recreation of a character's identity are developed. This relationship and dialogue invite the reader to make connections between the characters and events in the various novels. Strong links are evident in some texts, while in others, they are more subtle. For example, in *Silent Dancing*, Cofer's sense of identity is connected to the memories of the people and places that have danced in and out of her life. The notion of memory also plays an important role in Rivera's reclaiming of identity by recalling, through the voices of the migrant farm workers, the collective memory of the Chicano culture. A more subtle connection, along these lines, can be made to Trino, as he hears echoes of his own identity in the voice of the poet Emilce Montoya. The influences of changing cultural and physical environments on one's identity are felt by the characters of young Flavio in *Spirits of the High Mesa* and Consuelo in *Call Me Consuelo*. A more subtle connection can also be made with the character of David in *Jumping Off to Freedom*, who must come to grips with the future changes that await him in the new and unknown physical, cultural, and political environment of the United States. And, David's life, as presented in *Jumping Off to Freedom*, under the oppressive conditions of an unjust political system, is similar to the unjust and oppressive life experiences of the characters in Rivera's novel, reflecting sociological influences on the shaping of the identities of the characters. Thus, through all of these stories, there are opportunities for readers to make intertextual connections between the characters and perhaps to discover similar ties between the characters' identities and their own.

Other connections between the texts include the explicit focus on the power of words. In both *Silent Dancing* and *Trino's Choice,* the authors relay powerful messages about the importance of learning to read, not just the words, but also the meanings in the words, as well as being able to express oneself through language. And, the power of the oral language tradition is exemplified in the *cuentos* told in *Silent Dancing* and in the rich, descriptive narratives and dialogue in the *actos* of *...y no se lo tragó la tierra.* Finally, stories highlighting three male protagonists, Flavio *(Spirits of the High Mesa),* David *(Jumping Off to Freedom)* and Trino *(Trino's Choice),* illustrate the struggle with inner conflict in these coming-of-age stories.

These examples are just some of my own intertextual links between the young adult novels highlighted in this book. When I reread the novels in the future, I am sure that other connections between the texts will present themselves, because that is the nature of the reading and rereading process. And, there are, no doubt, many different connections that you and your students will make to these novels as well as other literary works that are part of your prior knowledge and experience. By adopting this intertextual approach to reading them, as readers, you and your students can create a connected network of meanings that will lead to a greater comprehension of texts and provide a broader base of knowledge and experience for future reading.

## Adapting the Strategies

As I stated earlier, when I first read the novels, each one seemed to naturally suggest the various strategies that are outlined in the respective chapters. My goal for developing each set of strategies has been to build a guiding framework that can help promote inquiry into the content of each novel and lead to deeper exploration of related topics suggested by that text. I have tried to include ways in which students can respond to the text through multiple modalities, incorporating a variety of content areas. This notion of a holistic approach in which disciplinary lines are blurred, along with multiple ways of expressing learning, can help students make stronger connections and develop better understandings in and across those content areas we have deemed important to include in the culture of schooling. However, these strategies do not necessarily need to be used in the order presented in the book and can be adapted for use across the texts, as well as with other literature studies you may implement in your classroom.

The following are just some examples of adapting the strategies to use with the other novels in this book.

First, there are some general strategies that can be used across all of the young adult novels in the chapters as well as with other literature studies. The formula poems, such as the *diamante* and the *biopoem,* provide ways to respond to the texts as well as synthesize learning about the different characters in each of the novels. The strategies, *Plotting the Plot* and *Casting the Characters,* which are found in Chapter 6 *(Spirits of the High Mesa),* can also be used with any text. Using drama to interpret and respond to literature is also adaptable to a wide variety of texts. Performance using *interior monologues,* such as those described in Chapter 7 *(...y no se lo tragó la tierra),* or *dramatic tableau,* as described in Chapter 4 *(Jumping Off to Freedom),* can actively engage readers in representing their learning in an alternative mode. And, the ethnographic strategies presented in *Silent Dancing* and *Trino's Choice,* along with the use of documentary photography, as discussed in *...y no se lo tragó la tierra,* as an ethnographic tool, can all be incorporated into inquiry projects that incorporate a variety of literature from different genre.

More specific adaptations of strategies might pair novels together. For example, in accord with *Identifying the Microcultures in Your School Setting,* found in Chapter 5, *Trino's Choice,* can also be used with *Call Me Consuelo,* Chapter 3. Likewise, the strategy of writing newspaper headlines described in *Read All About It,* found in Chapter 4, *Jumping Off to Freedom,* can be applied to writing headlines about the burglaries in *Call Me Consuelo.*

These are just a few suggestions about how you can adapt and apply the strategies presented in this book. Above all, keep in mind, they are all intended as examples, points of departure, and I hope you build on them so that they will reflect your own creativity and fit into your unique classroom context.

## The Relationship between Caring and Being Culturally Responsive

To be sure, the use of relevant materials is an integral part of culturally responsive instruction—one supports the other to create a teaching/learning environment necessary to fully develop a culturally responsive pedagogy. However, before we can begin to develop such a pedagogy, we, as teachers, must first adopt and develop a critically reflexive stance from which we can examine our attitudes, values, and understandings about teaching and learning with students from diverse cultural, linguistic, social, ethnic, and racial backgrounds. This is a continual meaning-making process, much like the transactional reading and rereading process described previously. This is important work, and it should be done often. From this reflexive stance, then, we can begin to build a fluid teaching and learning environment that supports a culturally responsive pedagogy. So, what does this environment look like, and what can we do to make it grow?

In thinking about what makes up such an environment, based on my own teaching experience and the conversations I have had with other teachers with whom I have worked, three important and necessary elements continually come to mind: trust, continuity, and reciprocity. These three important elements also characterize relationships that are built on what Noddings (1984; 1992) has defined as an ethics of caring. For Noddings, relationships between teachers and their students require a foundation built on trust. I think most teachers would agree that without a climate of mutual respect, there can be no trust established. Building trust is dependent on continuity of place, people, purpose, and curriculum. In other words, constancy over long periods of time is required for relationships to grow. In my experience, the presence of these two elements, trust and continuity, must be in place for the third, reciprocity, to occur and develop.

Noddings (1984; 1992) describes reciprocity in terms of a caring relationship between the carer and the cared-for. These are not fixed, permanent relationships, and the members can, and often do, exchange roles as different opportunities for caring arise. This relationship seems very parallel to the notion of Vygotsky's ZPD that I set out earlier, in which the teaching/learning relationship is fluid and the construction of meanings is a collaborative venture in which both parties are active contributors. Both caring and learning relationships depend on two important parts. First is the engagement and attention to the needs of others, which is demonstrated by the carer in Noddings's notion of care, and the scaffolder, in the Vygotskian notion of learning. Second, is the reception and responsiveness to that attention by the cared-for, or one who is being scaffolded. Now, here is where you are going to raise the question "What about the student who is not responsive, who is totally disengaged, who is failing in school, who just won't do the work, even though I really care about him or her?" I do not think answers can be found in a simple step-wise formula, because the nature of caring and learning is based in the notion of a dynamic relationship. Rather, seeking solutions depends on continually taking a reflexive look for possible disconnections that may have occurred in these defining elements. If we do not attend to these vital elements, all of which work together and support one another, we may experience breakdowns in the caring/teaching/learning relationship.

In our present culture of schooling, continuity can be an inherent difficulty. We are constantly faced with little time for coverage of a broad range of material, which is often characterized by a universalized knowledge base that has been deemed something everyone needs to know and be able to do. Now, I am not suggesting that we do not need to develop important cognitive and metacognitive strategies necessary for students to gain access to fundamental content knowledge. However, what I am suggesting, and what has been the guiding principle for this book, is that there are multiple avenues to accomplish these tasks. We need to help our students gain access to how to think—to be able to get at content and construct meaning through strategies that they can put into use, directing their own learning, without our direct intervention. Taking this kind of approach to instruction can provide a framework of continuity for students that can transcend the limited time and space of schooling. This kind of continuity promotes and nurtures trust—a trust that is built on respect for the other person, which includes a respect for his or her knowledge and experience. If we allow students to demonstrate their existing knowledge and use their unique experiential background to approach learning, alternative pathways to new knowledge and experiences can be built. It is only when we recognize and support the notion that each person has valuable knowledge and experience to contribute that reciprocity in the teaching/learning/caring relationship will occur. Developing and maintaining a learning environment and community of care, built on trust, continuity, and reciprocity, is necessary to a culturally responsive pedagogy.

## Closing Remarks

It seems appropriate to end our journey together with words from a classroom teacher that summarize, in a much better way, what I have been trying to describe in this book. I spent many hours listening, watching, and talking with Yvonne and her students about teaching and learning, and the relationships that flourished in their classroom seem to exemplify the kinds of relationships and environment described above. For Yvonne, many of her students were like "puzzling pieces whose edges did not mesh with the culture of school." These were the kids that "may not make it in an environment where success is defined by uniformity and everyone is traveling on the same road and getting there at the same time." In her view, "if you don't tend to and care for these children, they will wither and die on the vine." But, for Yvonne, caring and nurturing does not mean a lowering of expectations. On the contrary, it means an expanding of expectations outward and upward. Caring means finding alternative pathways to teaching and learning. Yvonne feels that one way to open up a path is by using literature that reflects the diversity of the students in your classroom. As she states, "When students can make connections with a text, when they can see themselves, their culture, their history, their circumstances and experiences in a story, they get involved in their learning, because it means something to them. When you think about it, in the bigger picture, that really means something to all of us." And, this is where the story continues.

# Works Cited

Alaska Native Knowledge Network. *Alaska Standards for Culturally-Responsive Schools*. Anchorage: n.p., 1998.

Atwell, N. *In the Middle: New Understandings About Reading and Writing*. NY: Boynton Cook, 1998.

Au, K., and C. Jordan. "Teaching Reading to Hawaiian Children: Finding a Culturally Appropriate Solution." In *Culture and the Bilingual Classroom: Studies in Classroom Ethnography*. H. Trueba, G.P Guthrie and K.H. Au. Eds. Rowley: Newbury House, 1981. 139–152

Barrera, R, and O. de Cortés. "Mexican American Children's Literature in the 1990s: Toward Authenticity." In *Using Multiethnic Literature in the K-8 Classroom*. V. Harris Ed. Norwood: Christopher Gordon, 1993. 129–153.

Bernardo, Anilú. (1996). *Jumping Off to Freedom*. Houston: Arte Público Press.

Bertrand, Diane Gonzales. *Trino's Choice*. Houston: Arte Público Press, 1999.

Bleich, D. *Subjective Criticism*. Baltimore: The Johns Hopkins University Press, 1975.

Bourdieu, P. *Distinction: A Social Critique of the Judgment of Taste*. Boston: Harvard University Press, 1986.

Bruce-Novoa, Juan. *Retrospace: Collected Essays on Chicano Literature*. Houston: Arte Público Press, 1990.

Calkins, L. *The Art of Teaching Writing*. Portsmouth: Heinemann, 1994.

_____, K. Montgomery, and D. Santman. *A Teacher's Guide to Standardized Reading Tests: Knowledge is Power.* Portsmouth: Heinemann, 1998.

Carspecken, P.F. *Critical Ethnography in Education Research: A Theoretical and Practical Guide.* New York: Routledge, 1996.

Clement, G. *Care, Autonomy, and Justice: Feminism and the Ethic of Care.* Boulder: Westview Press, 1996.

Cofer, Judith Ortiz. *Silent Dancing: A Partial Remembrance of a Puerto Rican Childhood.* Houston: Arte Público Press, 1990.

Coles, G. *Misreading Reading: The Bad Science that Hurts Children.* Portsmouth: Heinemann, 2000.

Crawford, J. Ed. *Language Loyalties: A Source Book on the Official English Controversy.* Chicago: The University of Chicago Press, 1992.

Daniels, H. *Literature Circles: Voice and Choice in the Student-Centered Classroom.* York: Stenhouse Publishers, 1994.

Dyson, A. H. and C. Genishi. Eds. *The Need for Story: Cultural Diversity in Classroom and Community.* Urbana: National Council of Teachers of English, 1994.

Fish, Stanley. *Is There a Text in this Class? The Authority of Interpretive Communities.* Cambridge: Harvard University Press, 1980.

Fiske, John. *Understanding Popular Culture.* New York: Routledge, 1989.

Freire, P. *Pedagogy of the Oppressed.* London: Penguin, 1972.

_____, and D. Macedo. Literacy: *Reading the Words and the World.* Westport: Bergin & Garvey, 1987.

Gay, G. *Culturally Responsive Teaching: Theory, Research, and Practice.* New York: Teachers College Press, 2000.

Geertz, C. *The Interpretation of Cultures.* New York: Basic Books, 1973.

Habermas, Jurgen. *The Theory of Communicative Action.* Thomas McCarthy, Trans. Boston: Beacon Press, 1987.

Harris, V.J. *Using Multiethnic Literature in the K-8 Classroom.* Norwood: Christopher-Gordon Publishers, 1997.

Hartman, D.K. "The Intertextual Links of Readers Using Multiple

Passages: A Postmodern/Semiotic/Cognitive View of Meaning Making." In *Theoretical Models and Processes of Reading (Fourth ed.).* Eds. R. Ruddell, M. Ruddell, and H. Sincer. Newark: International Reading Association, 1994. 616-636.

Heath, S.B. *Ways with Words: Language, Life, and Work in Communities and Classrooms.* Cambridge: Cambridge University Press, 1983.

Iser, W. *The Act of Reading: A Theory of Aesthetic Response.* Baltimore: Johns Hopkins University Press, 1978.

Kanellos, Nicolás. "Language and dialogue in ...*y no se lo tragó la tierra.*" In *International Studies in Honor of Tomás Rivera.* Ed. Julián Olivares. Houston: Arte Público Press, 1986. 53–65.

Kohn, A. *The Case Against Standardized Testing: Raising the Scores, Ruining the Schools.* Portsmouth: Heinemann, 2000.

Lachtman, Ofelia Dumas. *Call Me Consuelo.* Houston: Arte Público Press, 1997.

Ladson-Billings, G. *The Dreamkeepers: Successful Teachers of African American Children.* San Francisco: Jossey-Bass Publishers, 1994.

Lankshear, C., and P. McLaren. *Critical Literacy: Policy, Praxis and the Postmodern.* Albany: State University New York Press, 1993.

Lipka, J. *Transforming the Culture of Schools: Yup1ik Eskimos Examples.* Mahwah: Lawrence Erlbaum Associates, 1998.

Martínez, Floyd. *Spirits of the High Mesa.* Houston: Arte Público Press, 1997.

Meyers, M. *Changing our Minds: Negotiating English and Literacy.* Urbana: National Council of Teachers of English, 1996.

Mohatt, G., and F. Erickson. "Cultural Differences in Teaching Styles in an Odawa School." In *Culture and the Bilingual Classroom: Studies in Classroom Ethnography.* Eds. H. Trueba, G. Gutherie, and K. Au. Rowley: Newbury House, 1981. 87–106.

Murphy, S. *Fragile Evidence: A Critique of Reading Assessment.* Mahwah: Lawrence Erlbaum Associates, 1998.

*National Assessment of Educational Progress.* Washington, DC: U.S. Department of Education, 2000.

*National Center on Educational Statistics.* Washington, DC: U.S.

Department of Education, 1997.

Nieto, S. *Affirming Diversity: The Sociopolitical Context of Multicultural Education.* New York: Longman, 1992.

———. "We Have Stories to Tell: Puerto Ricans in Children's Books." In *Using Multiethnic Literature in the K-8 Classroom.* Ed. V. Harris. Norwood: Christopher Gordon, 1997. 59–93.

Noddings, N. *The Challenge to Care in Schools: An Alternative Approach to Education.* New York: Teachers College Press, 1992.

———. *A Feminine Approach to Ethics and Moral Education.* Berkeley: University of California Press, 1984.

Powell, R., S. C. Cantrell, and S. Adams. "Saving Black Mountain: The Promise of Critical Literacy in a Multicultural Democracy." *The Reading Teacher* 54 (2001): 116–132.

Rivera, Tomás. *...y no se lo tragó la tierra/And the Earth Did Not Devour Him.* Houston: Arte Público Press, 1996.

Rogers, T. "No Imagined Peaceful Place: A Story of Community, Texts, and Cultural Conversations in One Urban High School English Classroom." In *Reading Across Cultures: Teaching Literature in a Diverse Society.* Eds. T. Rogers and A. Soter. New York: Teachers College Press, 1997. 95–115.

Rosenblatt, L. M. *The Reader, the Text, the Poem: The Transactional Theory of the Literary Work.* Carbondale: Southern Illinois University Press, 1978.

Samway, K. D., and G. Whang. *Literature Study Circles in a Multicultural Classroom.* York, ME: Stenhouse Publishers, 1995.

Short, K. G., and K. M. Pierce. *Talking About Books: Creating Literate Communities.* Portsmouth: Heinemann, 1998.

Slapin, B., and D. Seale. *Through Indian Eyes: The Native Experience in Books for Children.* Philadelphia: New Society Publishers, 1992.

Soter, A. O. *Young Adult Literature and the New Literary Theories: Developing Critical Readers in Middle School.* New York: Teachers College Press, 1999.

Taylor, D. *Beginning to Read and the Spin Doctors of Science: The Political Campaign to Change America's Mind About How Children*

*Learn to Read.* Urbana: National Council of Teachers of English, 1998.

Tomlinson, C.M., and C. Lynch-Brown. *Essentials of Children's Literature* (4th ed.). Boston: Allyn and Bacon, 2002.

Tripp, D. "Critical incidents in action inquiry." In *Being Reflexive in Critical Education and Social Research.* Eds. G. Shacklock and J. Smyth. London: Falmer Press, 1998.

Vygotsky, L. S. *Mind in Society.* Cambridge: Harvard University Press, 1978.

Wertsch, J. V. *Voices of the Mind: A Sociocultural Approach to Mediated Action.* Cambridge: Harvard University Press, 1991.

# Bibliography

## Resources for Teachers

Abalos, David T. *Latinos in the United States: The Sacred and the Political.* SouthBend: University of Notre Dame Press, 1986.

Aliotta, Jerome J. *The Puerto Ricans.* New York: Chelsea House, 1991.

Boorstin, Daniel J., Brooks Mather Kelley with Ruth Frankel Boorstin. *A History of the United States.* Lexington: Ginn and Co, 1981.

Boswell, Thomas D., and James R. Curtis. *The Cuban American Experience: Culture, Images, and Perspectives.* Totowa: Rowman and Allanheld, 1984.

Bruce-Novoa, Juan. *RetroSpace: Collected Essays on Chicano Literature.* Houston: Arte Público Press, 1990.

Fernández, Alfredo A. *Adrift: The Cuban Raft People.* Houston: Arte Público Press, 2000.

Ferriss, Susan, and Ricardo Sandoval. *The Fight in the Fields: César Chávez and the Farmworkers Movement.* New York: Harcourt Brace, 1997.

Flores, Juan. *Divided Borders: Essays on Puerto Rican Identity.* Houston: Arte Público Press, 1993.

Flores, Judith LeBlanc. *Children of La Frontera: Binational Efforts to Serve Mexican Migrant and Immigrant Students.* Charleston: Appalachia Educational Laboratory, 1996.

Gann, Lewis H., and Peter J. Duignan. *The Hispanics in the United States: A History.* Boulder: Westview Press, 1986.

Gonzales, Rodolfo "Corky." *Message to Aztlán.* Houston: Arte Público Press, 2001.

Grillo, Evelio. *Black Cuban, Black American: A Memoir.* Houston: Arte Público Press, 2000.

Hammerback, John C., and Richard J. Jensen. *The Rhetorical Career of César Chávez.* College Station: Texas A & M University, 1998.

Heyck, Denis Lynn Daly. Ed. *Barrios and Borderlands: Cultures of Latinos and Latinas in the United States.* New York: Routledge, 1994.

Kanellos, Nicolás, and Claudio Esteva Fabregat. *Handbook of Hispanic Culture of the United States.* Houston: Arte Público Press, 1994.

_____. *Herencia: The Anthology of Hispanic Literature of the United States.* NY: Oxford University Press, 2002.

Mraz, John, and Jaime Vélez Storey. *Uprooted: Braceros in the Hermanos Mayo Lens.* Houston: Arte Público Press, 1996.

Olivares, Julián. Ed. *International Studies in Honor of Tomás Rivera.* Houston: Arte Público Press, 1986.

Ripoll, Carlos. *José Martí, the United States, and the Marxist Interpretation of Cuban History.* New Brunswick: Transaction Books, 1984.

Rosales, F. Arturo. *Testimonio: A Documentary History of the Mexican-American Struggle for Civil Rights.* Houston: Arte Público Press, 2000.

Rouse, Irving. *The Taínos: Rise and Decline of the People Who Greeted Columbus.* Binghamton: Vail-Ballou Press, 1992.

Saldívar, José David. Ed. *The Rolando Hinojosa Reader: Essays Historical and Critical.* Houston: Arte Público Press, 1985.

Sánchez, George J. *Becoming Mexican American: Ethnicity, Culture and Identity in Chicano Los Angeles, 1900–1945.* New York: Oxford University Press, 1993.

Suárez, Virgil. *Spared Angola: Memories from a Cuban-American Childhood.* Houston: Arte Público Press, 1997.

Suchlicki, Jaime. *Cuba: From Columbus to Castro.* Washington, D.C.: Pergamon-Brassey's, 1986.

Tijerina, Reies López. *They Called Me "King Tiger"; My struggle for the Land and Our Rights.* Houston: Arte Público Press, 2000.

Valdés, Guadalupe. *Con respeto: Bridging the Distances Between Culturally Diverse Families and Schools: An Ethnographic Portrait.* New

York: Teachers College Press, 1996.

Valdez, Luis. *Zoot Suit and Other Plays*. Houston: Arte Público Press, 1992.

## Bibliography of Suggested Young Adult Literature

Anaya, Rudolfo. *Bless me, Ultima*. Albuquerque: University of New Mexico Press, 1995.

_____. *The Heart of Aztlán: A novel*. Albuquerque: University of New Mexico Press, 1988.

_____. *Tortuga: A novel*. Albuquerque: University of New Mexico Press, 1998.

Aparicio, Frances. *Latino Voices*. Brookfield: Millbrooke Press, 1994.

Atkin, S. Beth. *Voices from the Fields: Children of Migrant Farmworkers Tell Their Stories*. Boston: Little, Brown and Company, 1993.

Ávila, Alfred. *Mexican Ghost Tales of the Southwest*. Houston: Arte Público Press, 1994.

Bencastro, Mario. *Odyssey to the North*. Houston: Arte Público Press, 1999.

Bernardo, Anilú. *Fitting in*. Houston: Arte Público Press, 1996.

_____. *Loves Me, Loves Me Not*. Houston: Arte Público Press, 1998.

Bertrand, Diane Gonzales. *Alicia's Treasure*. Houston: Arte Público Press, 1996.

_____. *Close to the Heart*. Houston: Arte Público Press, 2002.

_____. *Lessons of the Game*. Houston: Arte Público Press, 1998.

_____. *Sweet Fifteen*. Houston: Arte Público Press, 1995.

_____. *Trino's Choice*. Houston: Arte Público Press, 1999.

_____. *Trino's Time*. Houston: Arte Público Press, 2001.

Carlson, Lori M. Ed. *Cool Salsa: Bilingual Poems on Growing Up Latino in the United States*. NY: Ballantine, 1995.

Castilla, Julia Mercedes. *Emilio*. Houston: Arte Público Press, 1999.

Cisneros, Sandra. *The House on Mango Street*. New York: Vintage, 1991.

Cofer, Judith Ortiz. *The Year of Our Revolution*. Houston: Arte

Público Press, 1998.

Copley, Rober. E. *The Tall Mexican: The Life of Hank Aguirre, All-Star Pitcher, Businessman, and Humanitarian.* Houston: Arte Público Press, 2000.

de Anda, Diane. *The Ice Dove and Other Stories.* Houston: Arte Público Press, 1997.

de la Garza, Beatriz. *Pillars of Gold and Silver.* Houston: Arte Público Press, 1997.

de Ruiz, Dana Catherine, and Richard Larios. *La Causa: The Migrant Farmworkers' Story.* Austin: Raintree Steck-Vaughn, 1993.

Durán, Mike. *Don't Spit on My Corner.* Houston: Arte Público Press, 1992.

Galarza, Ernesto. *Barrio Boy.* University of Notre Dame Press, 1971.

García, Pelayo "Pete." *From Amigos to Friends.* Houston: Arte Público Press, 1997.

Hernández, Irene Beltrán. *Across the Great River.* Houston: Arte Público Press, 1989.

_____. *Heartbeat Drumbeat.* Houston: Arte Público Press, 1992.

_____. *The Secret of Two Brothers.* Houston: Arte Público Press, 1995.

Hernández, Jo Ann Yolanda. *White Bread Competition.* Houston: Arte Público Press, 1997.

Jiménez, Francisco. *Breaking Through.* Boston: Houghton Mifflin, 2001.

_____. *The Circuit: Stories from the Life of a Migrant Child.* Albuquerque: University of New Mexico Press, 1997.

Lachtman, Ofelia Dumas. *The Girl from Playa Blanca.* Houston: Arte Público Press, 1995.

_____. *Leticia's Secret.* Houston: Arte Público Press, 1997.

_____. *The Summer of El Pintor.* Houston: Arte Público Press, 2001.

Markusen, Bruce. *The Orlando Cepeda Story.* Houston: Arte Público Press, 2001.

Martí, José. *Versos sencillos/Simple Verses.* Houston: Arte Público Press, 1997.

Martínez, E. C. *Coming to America: The Mexican American Experi-*

*ence.* Brookfield: Millbrook Press, 1995.

Martínez, Víctor. *Parrot in the Oven: Mi vida.* NY: Harper Trophy, 1998.

Mohr, Nicholasa. *El Bronx Remembered.* Houston: Arte Público Press, 1989.

_____. *In Nueva York.* Houston: Arte Público Press, 1993.

_____. *Nilda.* Houston: Arte Público Press, 1991.

Mora, Pat. *My Own True Name: New and Selected Poems for Young Adults 1984-1999.* Houston: Arte Público Press, 2000.

Morales, Dionisio. *Dionicio Morales: A Life in Two Cultures.* Houston: Arte Público Press, 1997.

Myers, Walter Dean. *Scorpions.* New York: Harper & Row, 1998.

Piri, Thomas. *Stories from El Barrio.* New York: Knopf Books, 1992.

Prieto, Jorge. *The Quarterback Who Almost Wasn't.* Houston: Arte Público Press, 1994.

Ryan, Pam Muñoz. *Esperanza Rising.* New York: Scholastic, 2000.

Soto, Gary. *Baseball in April, and Other Stories.* San Diego: Harcourt Brace Jovanovich, 1990.

_____. *Buried Onions.* New York: HarperTrophy, 1999.

_____. *Local News.* San Diego: Harcourt Brace, 1993.

_____. *Pacific Crossing.* San Diego, CA: Harcourt Brace Jovanovich, 1992.

_____. *Taking Sides.* San Diego: Harcourt Brace Jovanovich, 1991.

Tashlik, Phyllis. Ed. *Hispanic, Female, and Young: An Anthology.* Houston: Arte Público Press, 1994.

Velásquez, Gloria. *Ankiza.* Houston: Arte Público Press, 2000.

_____. *Juanita Fights the School Board.* Houston: Arte Público Press, 1994.

_____. *Maya's Divided World.* Houston: Arte Público Press, 1995.

_____. *Rina's Family Secret.* Houston: Arte Público Press, 1998.

_____. *Tommy Stands Alone.* Houston: Arte Público Press, 1995.

Villaseñor, Víctor. *Walking Stars.* Houston: Arte Público Press, 1994.

Walker, Robert Paul. *Pride of Puerto Rico: The Life of Roberto Clemente.* San Diego: Harcourt Brace Jovanovich, 1998.